To My Darling Dee.
You continue to amaze and inspire
me.

.Acts of
inspiration

Justina Wokoma

The
X
Press

Published by
The X Press, 6 Hoxton Square, London N1 6NU
Tel: 0171 729 1199   Fax: 0171 729 1771

Distributed by Turnaround, Unit 3, Olympia Trading Estate, Coburg Road, London
N22 6TZ
Tel: 0181 829 3000   Fax: 0181 881 5088

Printed by Caledonian International Book Manufacturing Ltd, Glasgow, UK.

ISBN 1-874509-42-5

Acknowledgments

This book is inspired by:
The Creator. Though I doubted you, you never doubted in me.
Thank you.
My Mother and Brother.
The X Press.
Sharon Cole, a forward moving and creative sister.

Introduction

We intend to express our individual dark-skinned selves without fear or shame... We know we are beautiful. And ugly too... We build our temples for tomorrow, strong as we know how, and we stand on the top of the mountain, free within ourselves.   **Langston Hughes**

Acts of Inspiration reveals what people of colour *really* need in their lives and how to go about achieving it. This series of meditations are your day-by-day guide to spiritual fulfillment and how to succeed in life with your culture and your integrity in tact.

WARNING: This is *not* a think and discuss book. *Acts of Inspiration* is a DO IT NOW book. *Acts of Inspiration* will get you to show your full potential and benefit from it.

Acts of Inspiration covers every topic that you will need to know on your journey in search of satisfaction. Whether it is business, social, friendship, family or relationships, *Acts of Inspiration* guides you through life with a mixture of the ancient wisdoms and truths that have inspired people of colour for generations.

But *Acts of Inspiration* is not just a book on 'meditations for people of colour'. It is also a history book of achievements by people of colour. It covers two thousand years of inspirational achievements across the diaspora. Be inspired by the role that everyone from Harriet Tubman to Sojourner Truth, Rosa Parks, Winnie Mandela and Diane Abbott have played in our history. This historical testament will be a continuous reference point for you and all your family. Discover the great scientific achievements of people of colour. Learn about our role in culture, politics and technology. Read on and be inspired!

Remember, *Acts of Inspiration* is about YOU and how you can be inspired. You can keep a day-by-day account of the improvements in your life, by spending a little time each day to focus your thoughts. Turn to the pages at the back of *Acts of Inspiration* where you can make your unique and personal contribution.

Achievements are only made possible by setting up goals and what better way for you to keep check on how well you're doing than for you to document your acts of inspiration. Who knows, this time next year I might be reading YOUR Acts *of Inspiration*.

January 1

1988: Barbados born accountant Jim Braithwaite, sets up his multi-media computer firm in Brighton, England. Now valued at £20 million.

Build your dreams, nurture them, lean on them.
But most of all, BELIEVE in your dreams.

Drag yourself out of the darkness of ignorance. Bathe yourself in the light of truth. You are the descendant of an unconquered, indomitable people. Sometime, somewhere, the blood of a great queen or an empress flows through your veins. Your birthright is worth more than a thousand worlds. Treasure it. Go through life with a bearing that is truly regal, despite the heavy load. You are the product of generations of love, faith and achievement. And the fate of coming generations depends on YOUR love, YOUR faith and YOUR achievement.

January 2

1876: African-American Daniel Hale William is born. Destined to become the first doctor to perform open-heart surgery.

The world is yours when you master the secret.

Open your mind and look within. Check out who you really are and you'll wonder why you haven't shown your full potential yet. Allow yourself the luxury of an adventure into your inner spirit, deep into the very core of your thoughts and hold tight for a surprise. Kick back, relax, close your eyes and drift into the forgotten world of your soul where nothing is impossible, a billion miles away from the hustle and bustle and stress of day to day living. Find a moment to take a deep breath and push the 'pause' button on your life while you take stock. Discover, deep down where you are most intimate with yourself, your fire/power, waiting patiently for you to affirm belief in yourself. Waiting for you to BELIEVE that nothing is impossible.

January 3

An ant found a crumb with a dab of jam on it but could not push it home. A bee flew by. The ant called out, "Bee, can you please help me get this crumb home?" The bee said, "I have my own work to do. I have to get this pollen back to my hive or the queen will be angry," then flew off. Then a beetle came by. Again the ant asked for help. The beetle took a bite out of the crumb saying, "There you are, ant, I made your burden lighter for you." A spider perched on a nearby branch had seen the whole incident. When the ant asked for help, the spider replied, "I will do more than help you. I'll take the crumb home. My family will enjoy it." Hearing this, the ant took a firm grip on the crumb and heaved and pushed and before long reached the ant hill. The spider commented wryly, "I KNEW YOU COULD ACHIEVE A LOT MORE THAN YOU THOUGHT."

1954: Norma Sklarek becomes the first African-American fully licensed female architect in New York.

Black women MEAN business.

January 4

You refused to be what they wanted you to be. YOU ARE WHO YOU ARE. There's nothing to be ashamed about. You may not be perfect, that's okay. Perfection is only the image fools torment themselves with. But you are black and you are a woman, those are reasons enough to be proud and cheerful. Shame is someone else's burden and, if the cap fits, let THEM wear it. We refuse to be repressed by it any longer.

1940: Hattie McDaniel becomes the first black film star to win an Oscar for her role as Mammy in *Gone With The Wind*.

One of the greatest gifts is forgiveness.

January 5

1859: Harriet Wilson's *Our Nig* is the first novel penned by a black woman to be published.

I AM A BLACK WOMAN
strong...
beyond all definition...
defying place, time and
 circumstance...
indestructible.
Look on me and be
renewed.

Mari Evans

*I know I am black.
Beautiful.
With meaning.*
Sonia Sanchez

January 6

1910: African-American film director William Foster establishes the Foster Photoplay Co. and begins producing short films.

My head whirls with thoughts, but every now and then I remember that there is so much more knowledge to know than I am accustomed to knowing, much more sights to see than I have ever seen, so much more love to give than I am accustomed to giving and more, much more, love to receive than I am used to receiving.

Wherever I go there I am.

January 7

In all the world and through all of time there will never be anyone who is anything like you. Not by emotion, insight, genetic fingerprint or even sense of humour. It makes no sense therefore to compare yourself to another unique being. YOU are your only comparison. Wherever YOU are, is where you should be according to your work. Love and accept the whole of yourself, appreciate the being that is hot and cold, that is capable of both love and anger. If you wish to change, do it in terms of your own standards. YOU are unmistakably you. Rejoice in that fact!

2980BC: Imoteph, great architect of the step pyramid in Saqqara.

No one can make you feel inferior without your consent. Never give it.

January 8

Sungura (Swahili for Rabbit) used to have four normal legs, a pretty tail and chose to live in the trees because of the wonderful view. The monkeys advised him to choose a strong branch, but Sungura didn't heed their words. A strong wind swept through the trees and broke the branch. Sungura fell to the ground. His tail snapped off and he broke his back legs. Again the monkeys advised him: "Go see the healer. She can correct your legs." "Not today. Maybe tomorrow," Sungura said, relaxing. His hind legs healed just as they had broken. Ever since, rabbits are born with crooked hind legs. Sungura learned his lesson. Now rabbits are alert and fast. They never put off until tomorrow what should be done today. If you have something to do, DO IT NOW!

1958: Cordillera Stewart born. Founder member of the British Society of Black Lawyers.

Never put off for tomorrow what you can do today.

January 9

1978: U.S. postage stamp issued to commemorate Harriet Tubman. Nicknamed the Black Moses, she led over 300 slaves to freedom.

How are we gonna make the Black nation rise? Agitate. Educate. Organize. Brother D.

In this spinning, tumbling world strength is knowledge, knowledge is strength. Power comes from knowing who you are, where you come from and where you are heading. Knowledge of ourselves and our ancestors ensures that we are ready to face life and will cope and come out at the other end having learned something more about ourselves and become a little stronger.

January 10

1996: 9-year-old leukemia sufferer Daniel De Gale, leads the fight to increase the number of black blood and bone marrow donors in the UK.

We don't have to be afraid of loving. This is not the time to be without touch. We need it now more than ever. Charlotte Sherman

Everyone needs some loving sometime. Everyone desires tenderness expressed through a partner's gentle caress, a long loving kiss. Everyone deserves to feel that magic touch, from someone special. A touch which massages the spirit and lightens the soul and fills the well of loneliness. You deserve that too. Dare to demand your needs. Aim to attain your demands. Settle for nothing less.

January 11

Life for me is straightforward, easy and good. I know what I want. I want the same things as my mother — the joy of the world. But that's not all. I have never been afraid to reach out for my goals and grab them. Not that success, for me, is sure, infallible. But just that reaching out and touching them is my rule.

1987: Rastafarian Mr Innis successfully sues London Transport over a discriminatory ruling. The court upholds the fact that Mr Innis's dreadlocks would not affect his ability to do his job properly.

If you don't call out, who will hear you?
African proverb

January 12

Each residual feeling of anger, frustration, disappointment or hate that consumes our passions is two steps backwards in life. The wrongs and betrayal done to us by other people, can become heavy weights in our hearts which hold us back from appreciating the many gifts which are there for us if we only let go. How can you know peace when anger rages in your chest? The act of letting go of hurt brings an end to our suffering.

1900: London gets its first black mayor, lawyer John Archer.

When you have always lived in Armageddon, what do you know about the time of still waters?
Linda Brown

January 13

1873: From shoe shining, Miffin W. Gibbs rises to become a judge and, eventually, is appointed Registrar of Arkansas, USA.

One thing is certain, our elevation in life is the work of our hands.
Martin Delany

God first made us what we are and then out of our own creative genius we make ourselves what we want to be. Let the sky and God be our limit, and eternity our measurement. There is no height to which we cannot climb by using the active intelligence of our own minds. Mind creates, and as much as we desire in nature we can have through the creation of our own minds. In your homes and everywhere possible you must teach the higher development of science to your children; and be sure to develop a race of scientists par excellence, for in science and religion lies our only hope. Never forget your God.

Marcus Garvey

January 14

1914-18: Dr John Alcindor, an early pan-African activist in the black British community, works for the Red Cross during World War I, healing the wounded and saving lives.

When I discover who I am, I'll be free.
Ralph Ellison

STOP! Take stock. Why are you expending so much energy? Has it got you any nearer to your goal? When will you have time to enjoy the fruits of your labour if you are constantly striving for the next goal? Pause for a moment while you think about it. Time spent on reflection is never wasted. Calmly assess the direction you are heading in. Life is too short for diversions on the road to nowhere.

January 15

Hate is just as injurious to the person who hates. Like an unchecked cancer, hate corrodes the personality and eats away its vital unity. Hatred destroys the man's sense of values and his objectivity. It causes him to describe the beautiful as ugly and the ugly as beautiful, and to confuse the true with the false, and the false with the true. Love is the most durable power in the world. This creative force is the most potent instrument available in mankind's quest for peace and security.

Martin Luther King Jr

1929: Dr Martin Luther King Jr born. Destined to lead the Civil Rights movement and to give his life for it.

"You can get it if you really want But you must try, try and try, try and try... You'll succeed at last."
Jimmy Cliff

January 16

Courage is an inner resolution to go forward in spite of obstacles and frightening situations. Courage breeds creative self-affirmation; cowardice produces destructive self-abnegation. Courage faces fear and thereby masters it; cowardice represses fear and is thereby mastered by it. Courageous men never lose the zest for living even though their life situation is without zest. Cowardly men, overwhelmed by the uncertainties of life, lose the will to live. We must constantly build dikes of courage to hold back the flood of fear.　　　　　*Martin Luther King Jr*

1893: Bessie Colman born. Destined to become the first African-American woman to obtain a pilot's licence.

Once you know where you came from, there's no limit to where you can go.

January 17

1924: African-American cancer research biologist Jewel P. Cobb born in Chicago.

He sends you a bouquet of flowers, as if the fragrance alone has the power to redeem all sins. You ask for commitment, he accuses you of trying to chain his soul. Hugs and kisses, he informs you, are not lifetime contracts of companionship. To hitch your star to uncertainty is like playing Russian roulette — you need it like you need a hole in the head. Plant your own garden and, with its roses, decorate your soul. You don't need anybody else, you can do it all by yourself.

You are already what you are searching for.
Rashad Field

January 18

1980: Levi Watkins Jr. is the first black doctor to implant an automatic defibrillator in the human heart.

Before we can move forward in life, each of us has to confront the ghosts from our past that still haunt us. For example, how often as children we felt belittled and undermined by adult behaviour towards us and uttered that immortal phrase, "I will never treat my children like that," only to find in later life that we are replaying the same roles over again, without breaking the chain of destructive and painful patterns we learned in childhood. In order to change these patterns of behaviour we must face down the ghosts of yesteryear. Empower yourself with self-love and wash those demons out of your life for good.

Which of us has overcome his past?

January 19

We cannot choose the position from which we start in life, but we can determine the direction we take thereafter. You may come from humble beginnings but from that moment the world is yours to command. Be proud if your parents worked two jobs and seven days a week and ten of you slept in one bed. For women of colour, greatness often comes through struggle and "making a way where there was no way." Focus on who you are, where you come from and where you want to go and, like light breaking through the darkness, good times will come. Remember, the difficulties we encounter enhance our character.

1985: Caryl Phillips's novel *The Final Passage* wins the Malcolm X prize for literature.

It isn't where you came from; it's where you're going that counts.
Ella Fitzgerald

January 20

Whatever you want to do, do it your way. You never know, it could be the best way. But do it ANYWAY! Whatever you want to be, be it. You cannot hide your individuality. Why should you? Your experiences and your perceptions are like no other. So then, let your life reflect what your soul already is, entirely, unmistakably YOU!

My Aunty Roachy seh dat it bwile her temper an really bex her fi true anytime she hear anybody a style we Jamaican dialec as "corruption of the English language." For, if dat be de case, dem shoulda call English language corruption of Norman French an Latin an all dem tarra language what dem seh English is 'derived' from.
Louise Bennett

January 21

If I know the purpose of a bread knife, I can better determine whether this in my hand is a good example of one. Likewise, to know whether you are living a good life, you must first discover your purpose. You may have already lived your whole life by it without realising, but that is for you to find out in quiet contemplation. Your purpose is your personal rod of truth. Purpose is not a goal that you have to attain. It is a direction. You can travel south for a long time, but there is always plenty of south still to go. The goals we achieve are inspired by our purpose. To be on course in life we must always be "on purpose".

January 22

Success depends on a combination of things including: thought, feeling and action. They are as interdependent as the three sides of a triangle. If we are to accomplish any task these three factors must be present. Thought initiates the process. Feeling maintains the thoughts and induces further consideration. Action is necessary to accomplish the task. Unsuccessful projects lack one or more of these three elements. Human nature being what it is, it's usually action!

January 23

We build walls to protect ourselves from the pain of having family, friends and lovers, but those very same walls restrict our emotional and creative growth. As much as it hurts, pain is a fundamental part of the human condition and we have to face it squarely and deal with it. Walls take a great deal of energy to sustain, energy we should be using to improve our lives. Pull down those 'walls of Jericho' in your life and hear the beating heart within. Tear them down and re-establish links with those who love you.

1700's: runaway Jamaican slaves, known as Maroons, join together to fight English and French plantation owners.

Survival is day to day. Grasp your spirit and learn to survive.

January 24

As we move into the new millenium, a certain quickening of the will is moving through the black community all over the world. Sons and daughters of Africa whose humanity itself has, by grace, survived what might have been utter devastation, are heralding a process of cultural renewal, development and, the rebirth of mastery and greatness. You are a fundamental part of this process. Climb on board as the train leaves behind four hundred-plus years of barely survival, so that you too can cross the threshold into the year 2000, a born-again African.

1866: Ceylon born seaman Kamal Chunchie, establishes the Coloured Men's Institute to assist impoverished seamen and their families in Britain.

One should wish to celebrate more than be celebrated.

January 25

1717: Elizabeth Caesar writes a petition for the release of her husband, John Caesar, from slavery. The court finds in her favour.

No race can accomplish anything until its mind is awakened.
Booker T. Washington

Each of us must reach a level of consciousness where we realise that we must take charge of our lives, otherwise life runs over us like a through train. Until then we are slaves to ignorance and become battered and weary like flotsam, tossed on the sea of history. Recapture your life and hold onto it tight but with enough flexibility to let whatever might happen, happen.

January 26

1944: Angela Davis, black feminist activist and writer, born. Leading black power spokeswoman in the 60s, 70s and 80s.
We spend too much time preventing the heart from beating out its power. And before we know it, time has eluded us.

What has passed you can do nothing about, the future is yet to be told. For posterity the past has already been etched onto the pages of the 'book of life'. The pages ahead are all blank. The ink is not dry on the present. The story is still unfolding. It is down to you to decide the plot, style, pace and mixture of characters. You wield the pen. As you write, remember that even when you are gone, the book will live after you. Make sure you fill its pages with love and goodness.

January 27

Every day you are alive is a day to be celebrated, a gift. Let no day in your life pass you by without you formally acknowledging it. Your life is wealth in abundance. You may acquire the treasures of the world, but life will match every one of them when morning has broken and a new day rises on the horizon. With so much to gain, one lifetime is too short. Imagine then the value of the wastage for every day that is dominated by worry and misery. It is unrealistic to expect to be happy every day of our lives, but to waste so much of this gift on negative emotions is a pitiful shame.

1975: First UK black feature film, *Pressure*, is made and self-financed by the Caribbean born partnership of Horace Ove and Sam Selvon. The authorities fear the film's impact and ban it for years.

De same smaddy yuh hear-so from gwine spread hear-so pon yuh! An dem-deh weh yuh hear-so bout, gwine hear-so bout yuh too!
Louise Bennett

January 28

You have not come this far in your life, through thick and thin and all the hardships, without the strength of faith. Faith is the courage to face the world with friendliness and a smile. This same faith which has guided you through pain and sorrow will not abandon you now as the uncertainty of a new day confronts you, but will stay by you in your moment of despair. But do not take your faith for granted. Attend to it daily. Give it nourishment. Revive it regularly, or it's flame will flicker and die.

1982: Joe Hart and Sam Springer establish Black Rights UK to offer legal advice.

You can't be nobody but who you are. That shadow wasn't nothing but you growing into yourself. You either got to grow into it or cut it down to fit you. That's all you got to make life with and to measure yourself against that world out there.
August Wilson

January 29

1987: Janet Adegoke becomes the first black female mayor of the London borough of Hammersmith and Fulham.

Your mind is like soil in which ideas and thoughts are planted. That is why you have to water it regularly with knowledge. When the seed of an idea is sown on the fertile mind it flourishes and produces a great harvest. The land of ignorance, on the other hand, is dry and barren like a desert. Very few things can grow there. Cultivate and tend to your plot. Nurture it. Then you will know what your life is worth.

Our most cherished and valuable achievements are the achievements of spirit.

January 30

1943: Paul Robeson plays *Othello* on Broadway, New York. It runs for 296 performances, a record, at the time, for a Shakespeare play in the States.

Two people suffer a tragedy, one crumbles under the strain while the other deals with it and moves on. Uncentred people free fall from one situation to another. Without something firm to cling to we are blown about like dust. But if we are rooted, we have a point from which we can try and make sense of what occurs to us. A centred, rooted person can cope well with all that life has to throw at them and survive. A centred, rooted person is someone who has cleansed their doubts with knowledge of self.

Go within each day and find the inner strength so that the world will not blow your candle out.
K. Dunbar

January 31

Like a tree is known by its fruits we are known by our deeds. In order to produce delicious, ripe fruit the tree must firstly be good. If your spirit is tortured and broken how can you expect what comes from within to be whole? If you have no love for yourself how can life be good, productive and loving? Nourish and tend to the spirit. A damaged and dying tree is useless to a farmer as is a broken spirit to YOU. Heal the wounds that are caused by lies, disappointment and rejection. Then and only then can you REJOICE IN YOUR FULLNESS.

1990: Jim Williams becomes first black Lord Mayor of Bristol, a former slave port in West England.

If you have no confidence in self, you are twice defeated in the race of life. With confidence you have won even before you have started.
Marcus Garvey

February 1

To live and to love and to create are interconnected. By seeking one, you get the other two thrown in and so the whisper of the spirit becomes a mighty roar. Life without love is no life at all. The key of life opens the door to love. At the very least, love yourself. And when you love or you are loved, you are full of life and filled with creative inspiration. You too can paint a 'Mona Lisa', you too can compose a 'No Woman No Cry', you too can write a 'Song of Solomon.'

1960: Black college students stage a sit-in at a segregated Woolworths lunch counter in N. Carolina, starting a wave of similar civil rights demos in the southern states of America.

Never be afraid of moments.

February 2

1885: African-American Sarah Goode receives patent for the folding bed. One of only a handful of women to register their inventions.

Each of us must travel alone daily into that still, deep, silent place within us, to purify our soul of unclean things. In the hustle and bustle of modern living, we barely find time to attend to the spirit within. Meditation will give you the stillness and composure you need in your journey to float on the sea of experience. These still moments will allow you to bring forth the fruits of your wisdom. Meditation develops the gifts of patience and clear thinking and, tranquility will be the cornerstone of your character.

Take time to spend some time alone.

February 3

1879: From barber to County Commissioner of Chicago, John Johnson dies leaving an estate valued at over $70, 000.

Doctors don't consider the spiritual element. When we are feeling low they call it depression, yet it could simply be our soul calling out in pain. When it comes to healing the sickness of the soul, you have to become your own doctor.

Health is not a condition of matter, but of mind.

February 4

A salt doll travelled for thousands and thousands of miles over land and through many countries. It finally came to the edge of the sea. It was fascinated and enthralled by this strange moving, shifting mass, unlike anything it had previously seen. The salt doll asked the sea, "Who are you?" The sea smilingly replied, "Come in and find out." So the salt doll waded in. The further in it went the more it dissolved, until there was only a tiny bit of it left. Before the last bit dissolved, the doll exclaimed in joy and wonder, "Now I *know* what I am!" KNOW WHO YOU ARE BEFORE YOU RUN OUT OF OPTIONS.

1913: Rosa Parks, civil rights activist, born. Her refusal to give up her seat on a segregated bus sparked off bus boycotts in America's deep South in the 1950s and highlighted Civil Rights issues.

Strive to make something of yourself; then strive to make the most of yourself.

February 5

Look within, you are beautiful. Who told you otherwise? We constantly compare ourselves to the 'ideal' images portrayed around us and conclude that we are inadequate. But beauty, true beauty, is much more than skin deep. Learn to appreciate the god or goddess that resides within and discover the universal truth.

1987: Aboriginal activist Rikki Shields leads a protest as the Queen launches Australia's bicentennial celebrations. Shields defiantly raises the black, red and gold Aboriginal national flag.

"Lively up yourself and don't be no drag."
Bob Marley

February 6

1889: Nancy Green becomes the trademark for Aunt Jemima's recipe. Her face is 'America's most famous' and is seen on packets of the products all over the country.

Believe in your convictions, even if it means being convicted for your beliefs.

Doing the right thing requires commitment to life. Doing the right thing is what we choose when we wake up to the fact that we have worth and capability. Doing the right thing is done in the here and now, by us, for us.

February 7

1817: Frederick Douglass born into slavery. Becomes a leading abolitionist, author and civil rights activist.

Brother, brother, there's far too many of you dying..."
Marvin Gaye

Being black does not stop you. Do not belong to that group amongst people of colour who believe that nature has somehow given them a lowdown dirty deal and who feel it appropriate to forever moan about it. Even in the helter-skelter skirmish that is my life, I am too busy reaching for the sky to concern myself with excuses.

February 8

Let your home be a healing place, and every room within that dwelling be one that enhances the spirit and comforts the body. Consciously decide to talk with each other rather than spending so much time watching TV. Reclaim your home, make it a temple for meditation and creative expression. Add plants to the rooms to increase the oxygen to your brain. Allow the spirit to take residence.

1865: Paul Bogle, an abolitionist, took part in Jamaica's Morant Bay rebellion against the British colonialists.

He who hopes fares better than he who wishes, and he who wishes fares better than he who disappears.
Moroccan proverb

February 9

Dare to be great! Humbleness of spirit is a good quality, but do not let it inhibit your creative powers. Dare to be great! Shout loud with your joy, follow your dreams, sing the songs that tell of great deeds, and of heroes and heroines. Dare to be great! Be brave enough to admit your defeats and lift up your successes on a plate, show what you have done. Dare to be great! Cherish the ones who come into your life with a heart filled with love and compassion, not malice. Dare to be great! Dream dreams of splendour and happiness, contentment and fulfilment. Dare to be great!

1996: Deon Hemmings, Jamaica's first female gold in the Olympics. Black athlete Denise Lewis, Britain's only female medallist.

Whatever you do, do like a church steeple; aim high and go straight.
Rudolph Fisher

February 10

1837: Black Canadians win the right to vote.

We must learn to support each other's inspirational endeavours. No matter what field we are in, the advancement of one means the advancement of us all. Each one that achieves adds to the wealth of the collective whole.

Big up to the positive brothas and sistas in the community who KNOW what time it is.

February 11

1975: Adam Wade becomes the first African-American to host a game show, *Musical Chairs*, on national television.

The only person holding you back is you! Emancipate yourself from mental slavery, then you too can spread your wings and fly. You are the prisoner and the jailer. Take the key of self-love and open the gates of self-denial.

Free your mind and your behind will follow.

February 12

At times we surprise ourselves with our daring. Either by speaking out, refusing to be put upon or simply by taking steps which will bring us closer to a sense of ourselves. We have taken the first steps, towards self-empowerment, then we stop. Why? Because we are not sure, we are afraid to change and act on our dreams or plans. Abandoned dreams soon turn to dust and pollute your temple within and no matter how hard you try, you may never cleanse the residue left by countless thwarted dreams. Brush aside your worries. Grab hope firmly by one hand and courage with the other, and ride on the coat tails of all your desires.

1905: W.E.B. Du Bois establishes the Niagara movement, a political group which is to become the forerunner of the National Association for the Advancement of Colored People.

Give yourself up, bones as well. (Take a chance!) Ndebele proverb

February 13

Statistic: Only 10% of the human brain is used.

If only 10% of the human brain is used, what percentage of our POTENTIAL do we exploit? Ever had an idea that you felt sure would work, revolutionise our lives? Yes! Well, where is it? What happened? Still pipe-dreams? How much of your POTENTIAL did you exploit today? Your ideas may not always succeed, but the effort and the wealth of experience you will gain by trying is immeasurable. From simple dreams, empires arise and fortunes are made. The world is crying out for you to make use of your POTENTIAL.

1926: Errol James born. He later sets up the first Caribbean self-help group in Leeds in the north of England.

If you don't know what's going on, then ask somebody who does. Child, black folk are on the move an' there ain't no stopping us now.

February 14

Test yourself: dream the impossible dream and see if you can make that dream come true. I have so many prospects on the horizon that the future holds no anxiety for me at all.

February 15

Women spend time rushing around helping others, coping with people's demands, fulfilling roles of mother, wife, lover, co-worker, friend and daughter. Women of colour are famous for being strong for those who depend on us, taking charge of the situation to such an extent that we neglect ourselves. We forget that WE need help, a shoulder to cry on, a person to offload on. It is often easier to be an agony aunt for everyone else and avoid the pain that we ourselves are feeling. Admit that you are not always strong. Seek help when you need it. By ensuring our own conflicts are resolved we are better able to confront the world and deal with the situations that arise. Denying our own true feelings is a weakness. True strength comes from facing our difficulties and dealing with them.

February 16

There is no greed that cannot be turned to generosity, no bitterness which cannot be replaced by kindness, and no anger that cannot become sympathy. There is no family argument that cannot be resolved, no financial dispute which cannot be settled. Likewise, hardship can become comfort and hatred can turn to love. In you lies the answer to all your troubles.

1773: Phillis Wheatley is the first published black female poet.

A child is to be treated very carefully.
Luganda proverb

February 17

My children all know that someone loves them and they're happy. I make sure that they're always clean, well fed and comfortable. I tell them how beautiful they are and what they can accomplish if they put their minds to it and get an education. And I tell them to be proud of their blackness, to be proud of one another and, to pull together.

1859: Sir Samuel Lewis becomes the first black man to be knighted by Queen Victoria of Great Britain.

He who has made a door and a lock, has also made a key.

February 18

1993: Toni Morrison wins the Nobel Prize for Literature for her book *Beloved*.

By facing our fears we score a victory and increase our self-esteem. When we start facing up to all that we have learnt to fear we may surprise ourselves and discover that we are smarter, more creative and, a much stronger person than we ever imagined.

He who asks the question cannot avoid the answer. **Cameroon Proverb**

February 19

1967: Emperor Haile Selassie I of Ethiopia sets aside a substantial amount of land in Shashamanie for returning Africans from the West to live on and farm.

With the march of modern technology, logic and science rule our lives. We have forgotten what our African forefathers taught us: to practice getting in touch with the intuitive side of ourselves and listen to and trust the inner voice, the gut instinct — 'women's intuition'. When we learn to trust our intuition, we remember how to feel as well as think, and strike a balance between the rational and the intuitive. RECLAIM YOUR ANCESTOR'S LEGACY.

The thing to do is to grab the broom of anger and drive off the beast of fear. **Zora Neale Hurston**

February 20

To confront ourselves we must differentiate between the role we play: mother, husband, son, daughter, employee, carer, and the real us. Some people base themselves upon their roles and have no wish to discover who they really are. Roles are like garments, transitory. Wear them or, just as easily, take them off. You are naked underneath. Facing up to your nakedness may be painful, but the realisation is liberating.

1919: W.E.B. Du Bois chairs first Pan-African Congress in Paris.

Make some muscle in your head, but use the muscle in your heart.
A. Baraka

February 21

The saying goes, you can't teach an old dog new tricks — in fact the opposite is true. It does not matter how old you are, or how set in your ways you might have become, if you thirst for something — a new skill for example — you can learn it. The desire to learn something new is what proves that we are really alive. Not just breathing, but LIVING! Like the saying goes, age ain't nothin' but a number!

1959: Berry Gordy Jr. establishes Motown Records, soon to be the world's most successful black record label.

Self-definition is intimately linked with empowerment.

February 22

1981: James Berry wins the UK National Poetry Prize for _Fantasy of an African Child_.

I don't know but I've been told, if you keep on dancing you'll never grow old.
Ms. S Sharp

Contradictions in our lives mean either we are looking at life in the wrong way or that there are possibilities we have yet to consider. Contradictions are a useful tool, they make us stop and think and give us a chance to examine those things that we have always held to be true and sacred. When we come up against contradictions we should not throw away our principles or teachings but use it to examine the values that we hold on to. The contradiction might reaffirm what we already believe to be true or it might cause us to question our thoughts and motives deeply. Either way, contradictions provide a way of re-connecting ourselves to our thoughts, hopes and beliefs.

February 23

1997: From sound system operator to international superstar, Jazzie B's north London outfit, Soul II Soul, have now sold 7 million albums and 20 million singles.

A happy face and a thumping bass for a loving race.

A, B, C, D, E. These are the elementary building blocks of language and communication, lovingly taught to us by our parents. Now that you are older examine your speech and vocabulary. Does it express what you mean or does it leave you with a feeling of not being fully understood? By not expanding our vocabulary we place constraints on our emotions. The word is power. Pick up a dictionary today (any edition will do). Learn a few new words every day, it will not only enlarge your vocabulary but also unlock that spirit within bursting to express itself.

February 24

Of all the time I spend in the day, the time I take to develop my own mind is the most beneficial to me. My mind's hunger for development seems to be insatiable and for every session I can feel the improvement in me.

4th century AD: Ezana, king of Aksum, extends boundaries and trade, mints coins, introduces vowels into the language.

Language expands the brain, increases one's knowledge bank, enlarges the world, and challenges the vision of those who may not have vision.

February 25

You have talked enough and planned enough. Now it is time to DO instead of just talking. REALISE instead of simply planning or else "too late" will be your cry. Continue on the path and, as you go, occasionally glance back at how far you have come. If you haven't made progress, TALK even less and DO even more.

1975: Grenadan born David Pitt is made a peer. First black British man to gain a peerage - Lord Pitt of Hampstead.

Get there, and you will then decide how to manage.
Kigexi proverb

February 26

1951: George Washington Carver monument opens in Missouri. The first monument to honour an African-American.

We are sometimes stubborn enough to think that our situation can be changed to our benefit without us having to change within ourself. Change inevitably leads to other changes, like the ripples caused by a pebble being dropped into still water. You cannot make an alteration in one area of your life without it affecting all the other parts. By seeing change in terms of your entire lifestyle and those who are around you, you begin to realise how intricately woven our lives are. Out of change — progress, growth and change again. Life is a continual process of change.

One does not cross a river without getting wet.
Zulu proverb

February 27

1950: Cy Grant sings the news in calypso on British TV.

We are too quick to criticise others. We convince ourselves that this is done out of kindness, when it is done in a spirit of malice. Those around us need love and guidance. While we are busy meddling in others' lives, there is no energy left to sort out the things that are going wrong in our lives. Set your own house straight before you look to your neighbour's.

Do not mend your neighbour's fence before looking to your own.
Tanzanian proverb

February 28

We blame the lack of money for all that has gone wrong in our lives. We daydream about unimaginable wealth. We believe that with unlimited cash we would be able to do more with our lives, help our friends and relatives better. Then we sit and wait for bags of money to fall out of the sky and into our laps. The truth is that we can improve the quality of our lives ourselves by simply making the effort. The Creator helps those who help themselves. When we kick back and wait for those winning lottery numbers to come up, we're on our own.

1992: Bill Morris becomes the first black leader of the Transport & General Worker's Union (T&GWU), Britain's biggest trade union.

One cannot count on riches.
Somali proverb

February 29

It's not about whether you're a buppie, bap or raggamuffin, we are in this thing together. And if you earn more in a week than I earn in a year, we're still in this thing together. So we shouldn't be fighting each other, we should be working together and helping each other. EACH ONE HELPS ONE.

1970s-1980s: Desmond Douglas is the top Briton in table tennis. A first for Black Britain.

If a single hair has fallen from your head, you are not bald.
Sierra Leone

March 1

1864: Rebecca Lee Crumpler, first African American woman to receive a medical degree.

You are weeping. I share your pain, I too have suffered. Who feels it knows it. Cry your tears, but please don't give up now. There is a light within you, so let it shine. Give it a try. Come on.

He who refuses a gift will not fill his barn.
Sierra Leone

March 2

1891: Wiley G. Overton is appointed as New York's first black police officer.

In order for a runner to reach the end of the race she must prepare long and hard before the race begins. Starting at the beginning, placing one foot in front of the other and keeping in a straight line. We must be as single-minded in our approach to tasks if we are not to be frustrated in our efforts. Each step will bring us closer to our goal. But if the steps we take are not consistent the goal will always remain in the distance. Consistent effort will bring us to the end, large steps here and there will move us, but many small repetitive steps will bring us to the end quicker and in a healthier mental state.

A paddle here, a paddle there - the canoe stays still.
Sierra Leone

March 3

Does it feel like just when you have picked yourself up and dusted yourself down, you get a blow that knocks you off your feet again? Be inspired. These setbacks, however wearisome, are there to test your faith. You are the descendant of men and women who faced more tribulation than it was thought that a person could manage. Yet they survived. They had faith. Let that be uppermost in your mind as you face that problem squarely and deal with it.

1785: Rev. G.W. Hobbs' pastel portrait of Richard Allen, a Methodist Minister, is the first known portrait of a black man.

A healthy ear can stand hearing sick words.
Senegalese proverb

March 4

Do you, like me, wonder where the statues and memorials are to the great heroes and heroines of colour throughout history? Do you, like me, wish you could do something to rectify the situation? Then now is your chance. A proper memorial to our great ancestors would be one in which we would dedicate and re-dedicate our lives to achieving their dreams of freedom, justice and love.

1987: Pauline Wiltshire publishes her autobiography *Living and Winning*, a harrowing yet compelling account of her experiences as a disabled black woman.

If a centipede loses a leg, it does not prevent him from walking.
Senegalese proverb

March 5

We are known by the deeds that we do, the things that we say, the impression people have of us. Are you are storyteller, a businessperson, an artist? These are your trade marks. Do you encourage people, make them laugh, show enthusiasm for their ideas? These are what you will be remembered by. The product of the heart is seen by all for what it is. The good and bad in you will always come out plainly for the world to see.

When you see an old lady running, do not ask what is the matter, run too.
Jamaican proverb

March 6

1909: Walter Tull is one of the first black footballers to play soccer for a professional English club, Tottenham Hotspur.

In life we have two rights: a) to succeed and b) to make mistakes. When we succeed we are fine, we pat ourselves on the back, blow our trumpet and generally feel very pleased with ourselves. When we make a mistake the hand that was patting us so kindly on the back we use to beat ourselves with. We personalise our mistakes until they almost cripple us and prevent us from trying again. We think that our mistakes are disasters and that they are beyond change or reconcilement. As people of colour we feel that we are under constant scrutiny and that we cannot afford to make any mistakes and, if we do, we are not only letting ourselves down but the race as a whole. Like everyone else, we are prone to flaws, but ultimately capable of great deeds. Remember that.

When you know who his friend is, you know who he is.
Senegal saying

March 7

Parents at a parent training course were asked, "What words would you use to describe your children?" 70% were negative: "My children are hard work, difficult, disobedient and willful." If this is what you think, your children will sense it and feel that they are a burden. And before you can say, "My kids are what makes life worth living," you will have ostracised them. Our children are the product of love and joy. Be proud of them and treat them with a degree of respect, even when they cause you difficulties. Where else are they to learn good relationship skills if not in the home? Love is the key.

1989: Ellery Hanley plays for and coaches the Great Britain Rugby League team.

The bird that flaps its wings too much will drop its feathers. (Generosity without limit will exhaust one's resource.)
Kikuyu proverb

March 8

Be good to yourself
Accept yourself — totally
Be yourself — confidently
Treat yourself — lovingly
Give yourself — completely
Bless yourself — generously
Forgive yourself — wholeheartedly
Value yourself — immensely
Balance yourself — harmoniously
Trust yourself — implicitly
Love yourself — completely
Express yourself — abundantly.

1945: Phylis M. Daley is the first African-American woman to serve in the U.S. Navy.

The revolution won't get rid of the tiger in your tank, nor the giant in your toilet bowl, but it WILL put YOU in the driver's seat.
Gil-Scott Heron

March 9

1962: Africa Centre, London, opened by President Kaunda of Zambia. Exhibiting African art, crafts and talent.

You're running and you're running away, but you can't run away from yourself. You can run in circles and end up exactly where you began, or run in a straight line to the end of the earth and, like a shadow, yourself is still right there beside you. Don't spend your life running away from yourself. Sooner or later you will tire of running and have to face yourself. Acknowledge that this is your destiny. The moment you stop running is the moment you start building your life.

The troubles that chase you away also show the road.
Kigezi proverb

March 10

1729: Ignatius Sancho's autobiography becomes a bestseller. The runaway slave taught himself to read and write, and became the first black prose writer to be published.

You are a shining example of a perfect human being. The good that you do is proof of that. The positive vibes that you exhude to all around you is the evidence. Only a perfect parent could have raised such wonderful children. No need to consider your 'perfect' nose or 'perfect' teeth, just take a look at all the smiling faces around you and remind yourself just how perfect you are — nappy hair and all.

"Got so much trouble on my mind...
I refuse to lose."
Public Enemy

March 11

Wherever you see a glass ceiling, crash through it. Nothing made of glass can hold you back unless, that is, you listen to those who say no way can you do that. Keep going on until you get to the very top of whatever you're doing in life, where you'll find a real ceiling — the heavens above. Meanwhile, no person born of woman (or scientific devices) can stop you from becoming the very best of the very best.

1845: Former slave Olaudah Equiano's autobiography, takes England by storm, it sells nine editions and influences U.S. abolitionist Frederick Douglass in his own writing.

Men will be gods if they want.

March 12

To actually do something about our situation requires us to expend energy. It seems easier to allow our needs to be overlooked — to starve — than to learn what we need and how we are to get it. When we do nothing and wait for the powers that be to do what they will, we opt to starve. Imagine a hungry worker in a field of yams who refuses to bend and harvest some. There is no way of assuaging their hunger without bending. If we feel starved of attention and affection, without reaching out we will not get them. We need to understand what we need and where we go to get it. Admitting that we have needs doesn't make us less of a person, emotional starvation does.

1980: After defeating Rhodesia's racist regime on the battlefield, Robert Mugabe leads Zimbabwe to independence. <u>Africans liberated Zimbabwe.</u>

Become concerned with complexity, and you will lose sight of simplicity.

March 13

Work, family, duty, love and friendship sometimes prevent us from enjoying life's simple pleasures. Commitments overwhelm us, yet we have to fulfill them. If you plan your day properly you will be able to meet all your commitments and still have time to rest, take stock, and notice the beauty of that rainbow for the first time, instead of spending the entire day chasing waterfalls. Get a diary. Plan your minute. Plan the hour. Plan your day. Plan your week. Plan the year. Plan your life.

MANY ARE THE BOOKS WHICH INSPIRE ME. HERE ARE JUST A FEW:

Invisible Man Ralph Ellison
The Women of Brewster Place Gloria Naylor
Their Eyes Were Watching God Zora Neale Hurston
Beloved Toni Morrison
Native Son Richard Wright
In Search of Satisfaction J. California Cooper
Black No More George Schuyler
The Salt Eaters Toni Cade Bambara
The Color Purple Alice Walker

Dark an stormy may come de wedder;
I jines dis he-male an' dis she-male togedder.
Let none, but Him dat makes de thunder,
Put dis he-male an' dis she-male asunder.
I darfore 'nounce you bofe de same.
Be good, go 'long, an' keep up yo' name.
De broomstick's jumped, de world's not wide.
She's now yo' own. Salute yo' bride!

Slave Marriage Ceremony

March 14

Every once in a while check in with yourself, see where you are going and what you have learnt in the meantime — talk to yourself. If we can do this and clearly define what OUR needs and aspirations are, we can do the same with others. Communication, the giving and receiving of information, the talk and the listen, is vital. When we express ourselves we let others know our needs, desires and dreams. Listening to the voice within is one of the most loving things we can do for ourselves.

MANY ARE THE RECORDING ARTSTS WHO INSPIRE ME. HERE ARE JUST A FEW:

Bob Marley

Stevie Wonder

Tracy Chapman

Marvin Gaye

John Coltrane

Billie Holiday

Public Enemy

Sounds of Blackness

Erykah Badu

They dragged you from the motherland, Chained you and huddled you in filthy hatches, then sold you.

They broke you in like oxen, scourged you, branded you, made your women breeders, They swelled your numbers with bastards... Then taught you the religion they disgraced.

*You sang: 'Keep a-inchin' along Lak a po' inch worm...'
You sang: 'Bye and bye I'm gonna lay down dis heaby load...'
You sang: 'Walk togedder, chillen, Dontcha git weary...'
And the strong men keep a-comin' on, the strong men git stronger*

March 15

1943: James A. Porter's book *Modern Negro Art* **is the first comprehensive study of African-American art.**

Make each day count. Live today for today. Tomorrow will come no matter what. Not every day will be filled with joy. Accept that like everybody else has to. Some days the bills will all come at once, your boss will get you down and you'll want to go back to bed and start all over again. Instead of trying to wish the day away, sort out the bills and face your job determined to do what it takes to get a better job as soon as possible. Now you can face tomorrow confidently and with a smile. What a difference a day makes!

Art is the soul of black folk.

March 16

1989: Medlin Lewis becomes the first black female mayor of the London borough of Hackney.

I used to fall hopelessly in love. Deep. But my heart has been broken so many times that what matters now is that I heal myself spiritually, physically and emotionally. I will do whatever it takes to feel whole again. Maybe one day, I will fall HOPEFULLY in love.

Every wish is like a prayer to God.

March 17

Life takes its time, yet we draw up timetables and lists of things we want to achieve by a certain date. We want to be married at a certain age, have our own home, children, or to have reached a certain level at work by such and such a time. We thereby prevent the river of life from taking us in any of a number of other directions. Allow things to be done in their natural time. Use the timetable of your life as a guide, nothing more, because a better option might be waiting just around the next corner.

1978: First black soap *Empire Road* aired on British television.

It's a long road, but I know I'm gonna find the end.
Bessie Smith

March 18

Revenge is sweet — or is it? Why do we want to exact retribution on those who have crossed us? Self preservation, or simply pride? Consider all the time you spend plotting and scheming for revenge, time that could be better spent doing something positive. You are supposed to be going forward, remember? If you want satisfaction for your grievance, then overcome your negative emotions and live well. Nothing will answer your foe better than your success and happiness in life. Smouldering fires can be rekindled, but the smouldering desire for revenge will turn your life into piles of ashes. If you still harbour resentment from past conflicts with friends, relatives and lovers find a way of resolving them, or simply abandon them. Leave them behind. Keep on moving. Put out the fire.

1966: New Beacon, first black book shop in London.

If there has been a secret to my success it's, don't take no for an answer when you must hear yes.
June Jackson Christmas

March 19

1875: UK black composer Samuel Coleridge Taylor born. Hailed as a musical genius, he compares to Beethoven, Brahms, etc.

*The blues help us laugh at our misfortune, and reaffirms that living is what life is about, no matter how many hurdles we have to jump. **Opal Palmer Adisa***

We have a great tradition of song, both of sorrow and of joy. Songs that helped us when the terrors of night matched the horrors of the day. Through those songs we told of our lives, our beliefs, our hopes and aspirations. We need only reach a short way back into ourselves and we will find that we have the words. Sing the song that tells of your day, your love and your child. Sing songs that tell of your hopes and fears. As you sing, your spirit will emerge to walk beside youu in your passage through life.

March 20

1917: UK's first black student's union launched. Its inaugral president is E.S. Beoku Betts from Sierra Leone.

A hole in the ground — do you walk round it, or try to jump over it? The sensible way: AROUND. Why not apply the same logic to the rest of your life? The relationship is bad, it degrades us, lowers our esteem and prevents us from moving on. Do we pack our bags and move on? Or do we linger, deluding ourselves that through some unknown fate the relationship will get better? The sensible way: WE KNOW WHAT WE WANT AND WHAT WE HAVE TO DO TO GET THERE.

We all know better, it's just hard to always do better.

March 21

Each of us is filled to the brim with untapped energy buzzing away inside. What will you do with yours? You can move mountains with it and you can part seas. Or use it to spend a little more effort loving somebody. Light the spark and you too will find that you have enough untapped power inside you to reach the stars. A soul on fire is a spectacular sight to behold.

1921: First major exhibition of African-American art is held at a branch of the New York Public Library.

I am a spark ready to burst into flame.

March 22

When we look back on our lives and think of those who have had a positive effect on us, we find that they always arrived in 'the nick of time' — just when we needed them and were able to appreciate them. They brought hope into our lives where there was none, they brought joy, wisdom and peace. Then we look back on our lives and think of those who have had a negative effect on us, those who brought pain, ignorance and disharmony. To me it seems obvious that, by any means necessary, I must stop negative people from finding a home in my world.

1996: With £1 million of his own money, heavyweight boxing champ Lennox Lewis sets up a school in east London for underprivileged inner city kids.

I'm a lover of black mothers. And black mothers need sons, not children who've been killed by guns.
Brand Nubian

March 23

1967: Caribbean born Dudley Dryden & Len Dyke set up a cosmetics business in London. It is now a multi-million dollar company.

It's not an easy road,
Many see de glamour an' de glitter so dem t'ink a bed ah rose
Who feels it knows...
Buju Banton

Worry drains your energy. The energy you are using to worry is diverted from coping with the things you are worrying about. We worry that our lives may be changing and about the new problems we may have to face. We worry that our lives aren't changing and we want it to. We worry to such an extent that as the day goes past, we haven't completed the things we had meant to do. Then we worry about that as well. We wake up worrying and go to sleep worrying, wishing we weren't worrying. Spend ten minutes less time worrying every day and see how much more you can achieve.

March 24

1968: Jamaican Everton Forbes is among the first travel agents to run UK charter flights to the Caribbean.

Walk good an' Good Spirit walk wid yuh through life, yuh see.
Caribbean proverb

When our lives are unfulfilling, we say life is boring. Boredom leads to restlessness and restlessness to action. We are galvanised into making changes. Superficial changes are easy (decorating our home, buying a car or taking a holiday), but have no lasting impact. Our lives still feel unfulfilled. Life is still "boring". Because we have not listened to the voice within which knows all the secrets of our soul. When you feel unfulfilled, your soul is looking for REAL change. It is already too late for cosmetic surgery, this patient needs to be rushed to intensive care immediately! Review the changes you have made to your life in the past year and whether you are satisfied. Listen carefully to that voice within and discover what your soul needs and change accordingly.

March 25

The Creator has given us many gifts. Time, however, is not a gift. We have it on loan. When we take time to contemplate, we can tap into our power within. When we take time to read, we bathe in the fountain of wisdom. When we take time to live a little, we discover the river of pleasure. And the time we take to love and be loved feeds us emotionally. But if you waste time, the Creator will take it back sooner than you expect.

1942: Aretha Franklin born. The daughter of a preacher, she is destined to become the 'queen of soul'.

Man is master of his own destiny and architect of his own fate.
Marcus Garvey

March 26

Surround yourself with people who inspire you and seek out those who will be inspired by you. Listen to inspirational speakers, exchange a word or two with them. Make your own inspiration and share it with others. To inspire and be inspired are amongst the great gifts of life. Make sure you have both in abundance.

1996: President Nelson Mandela of South Africa is given a hero's welcome when he visits Brixton at the heart of London's black community, to thank residents for their contribution to the anti-apartheid struggle and his release from jail. *Amandla!*

March 27

21st century:
Black population
in London.
1948 - 3,200
1950 - 4,500
1952 - 12,200
1955 - 15,000
1956 - 28,000
1957 - 41,000
1958 - 40,000
1959 - 51,000
1960 - 60,000
1962 - 135,000
2020 - 2 million
(estimated)

*One may receive
the information
but miss the
teaching.
Jean Toomer*

We are born into the school of life. We learn more in those first few years than we'll every learn again, especially about ourselves. Every minute, every second of a child's day is spent learning. As we grow older we get into the habit of learning part-time. By adulthood we think that we know all there is to know. We couldn't be further from the truth. See how strong your child grown every day. Can't you see that KNOWLEDGE IS POWER?

March 28

1826-1884:
Cetawayo,
King Of
Zululand,
ruled with
insight and
wisdom. The
English and
Dutch
colonialists
suffered great
defeats at his
hands.

*Learn the rope
of life by
untying its
knots.*

Who or what is the teacher of life? The only true answer is YOU. You are the one who decides what you are exposed to, what is rejected. At best, life can only present you with lessons. The rest is up to you. Each of us is a teacher. Through the calamities of life, let us teach ourselves that "I am always here, always have been, always will be, no matter what."

March 29

The lives of so many of my sisters-in-spirit contain the same sad themes of unfulfilled longings and deep inner frustration. Rarely do they feel the rhythmic enchanting vibrations of life, nor hear the mystic sympathetic tones of nature's aeolian harp. Unfulfilled desires drain our emotional well of creativity, until it finally dries up completely. Realise your desires and quench your thirst.

1963: Paul Stevenson organises a bus boycott against a bus company after they introduced a colour bar in Bristol, west England.

People cling to their hates so stubbornly because they sense, once hate is gone, that they will be forced to deal with pain.
James Baldwin

March 30

Make a sacrifice. Give it up, throw it away, go cold turkey, kick it to the curb! Why are you hanging on to that vice? You must go that extra step to have a better quality of life. Don't wait until New Year to make that resolution, do it now.

1463: Sonni Ali born in Africa. A soldier, he rose through the ranks to become the commander of an empire the size of Europe.

If you have no confidence in self, you are twice defeated in the race of life.
Marcus Garvey

March 31

1820: James Warton, a cabin boy, rises to boxing fame in London by winning all his nine prize fights, the most famous of which lasted 200 rounds.

You are direct and self-accepting as a lion in African velvet.
Gwendolyn Brooks

Women at a seminar were asked what they were looking for in a partner. One lady stood up and listed the attributes she most desired. "A tall distinguished gentleman. A man who would sweep me off my feet, lavish me with presents, constantly surprise me. Be extremely romantic, take me to the best shows, film premieres and performances with the best seats in the house. Naturally!" When she had finished her litany another member of the group commented, "You don't want a husband, you want a cheap romance novel."

April 1

1995: UK journalist Onyekachi Wambu, launches African Remembrance Day to honour the millions of mothers, fathers and children lost on the middle passage.

The black man, original man, built great empires and civilisations and cultures while the white man was still living on all fours in caves.
Malcolm X

Remember, our ancestors built great cities and ruled vast empires. They also produced exquisite crafts. Were great scientists and mathematicians. Invented tools to aid farming. Discussed politics, studied the constellations and navigated the seas aided by instruments of greater accuracy than those elsewhere. These are the men and women from whom we have descended. In honour of their memory and the legacy they have left us, we must build on their solid foundations and create our own legacy that, in turn, our descendants may look upon and marvel at with pride.

April 2

For each of us there may come a time when we will have to take a stand, a moment when we will have to make a hard decision that may change our lives forever. It may be that you will have to stand up and say things that need to be said. Or you may have to shed that heavy load you've been carrying for far too long. You may need all your courage, tenacity, perseverance, assertiveness, intelligence, talents, blessedness, feistiness and nerve. But once you've opened that door walk through it, don't look back, or you may miss that great 'turning point' of your life.

1881: Arthur Wharton, the first black footballer in Britain is already playing for Preston North End when the Football League is established.

Knowledge is the prime need of the hour.
Mary McLeod Bethune

April 3

A child looks around and asks questions: "Why is the sky blue, the sun yellow, the grass green? Where does the wind come from and where does it go? How do animals know when to get up and what to eat?" With each question comes another and a greater sense of understanding and puzzlement. By the time we become adults we have seen the sun rise and set a thousand times. We have watched lightning strike and seen snow flakes fall so often it no longer leaves us in awe. Our eyes have become accustomed to these and other sights and our heart no longer thrills at them. The passing of time should not dull our senses to the spectacles of life. Each new day has dawned in its own special way. Every time we close our eyes to the pleasures each new day offers, a part of our spirit dies.

1966: Robert C. Weaver becomes the first black member of the US cabinet, as Secretary of Housing and Urban Development under Lyndon Johnson.

To me, the whole world is a place of wonder.

April 4

1928: Inspirational writer Maya Angelou born.

Your kids will have a number of friends throughout their lives but only one mother and father. Have the courage to be a parent.
Denise L. Stinson

The greatest legacy a parent can leave a child is the feeling of being loved. The relationships we have at home determine the kind that we will have in the world. By ensuring that we nurture our children's spirits and build a strong and abiding bond with them, we produce adults who are confident, centred, loving and happy. They will, in turn, pass that light of love onto those around them. Without a good template, what do we have to work with?

April 5

1826: African-American Henry Boyd, establishes a successful bed frame and furniture business.

Let us not try to be the best or worst of others, but let us make the effort to be the best of ourselves.

It's time to honour black men and women who have made their distinct contributions to our history. Sojourner Truth is worthy of sainthood alongside Joan of Arc; Crispus Attucks and George William Gordon, with no less glory than that of the martyrs of any other race. Toussaint L'Ouverture's brilliancy as a soldier and statesman outshone that of Cromwell, Napoleon and Washington. He is entitled to the highest place as a hero among men. Africa has produced countless numbers of men and women, in war and in peace, whose lustre and bravery outshine that of any other people. So why do we not acknowledge them? We must inspire a doctrine of our own without any apologies to the powers that be.

April 6

When we look in the media, we often see distorted and incorrect images of ourselves. If our spirit is not to be crushed by these bogus depictions, we must challenge every false prophet who portrays us inaccurately. That's the way to make the black nation rise. For every image of black failure, a thousand black successes are ignored to diminish our sense of self worth. For every instance of lawlessness in our community, there are countless upstanding citizens making positive contributions. It is our responsibility to seize these positive images and demand they be promoted in our books, newspapers, radio and TV shows.

1992: Black Alcohol Workers Forum established as the first help group for black people with alcohol related problems.

Monitor the images your children are exposed to on TV for those that tell them that as people of colour they are not beautiful, desirable, smart or good.
Denise L. Stinson

April 7

It's time to clear out the wardrobe of your soul. Time for a spring cleaning of your life. Some of the things you used to enjoy will no longer appeal. But don't be alarmed. You have changed. Everything changes. Simply change to something better. Dust the cobwebs and look into the luggage you carry with you every day and see what has passed its 'use by' date. The sooner you get rid of that, the sooner you'll be able to carry on with the rest of your life.

1890: Ida Gray graduates from the University of Michigan Dental School, and establishes a dental practice in Cincinnati.

When visitor come ah me fireside, me mek me pot smell sweet.
Jamaican proverb

April 8

1801:
Toussaint
L'Ouverture
leads
Haitians to
defeat the
French army.

God give us leaders!

"Where are our great leaders?" Why has nobody filled the shoes of Malcolm X, Martin Luther King Jnr, Marcus Garvey, Harriet Tubman, Kwame Nkrumah? Times like these demand strong minds, great hearts, true faith and ready hands:

Leaders whom the lust of office does not flatter.
Leaders whom the spoils of life cannot buy.
Leaders who possess opinions and a will.
Leaders who are honourable.
Tall leaders, sun crowned, who live above the fog in public duty and private thinking.
"Where are our great leaders?"

What we need in the race are mental and spiritual giants who are aflame with a purpose. That means YOU!

April 9

*1914:
Chief Sam,
nicknamed
'The Gold
Coast
Messiah', buys
a ship to help
return black
Americans to
Africa.*

How hungry are we for love? Hunger is not only lack of physical nourishment, but also spiritual starvation. The hunger for LOVE is so deep, so powerful, to ignore it could have grave consequences. Without love we become self-centred and bitter. If the spirit is not fed with love it will die. With love, we move forward tirelessly.

One thing nobody can deprive you of - imagination.

April 10

Automatic, push button, remote control, synthetic genetics command your soul. We are slaves to science when we should be its masters. It is up to you to make yourself familiar with new methods of communication and technology. After all, it should come as second nature. Weren't your forbears the ones who first calculated mathematics? Didn't your ancestors use physics to build glorious temples when other people's ancestors were crawling in caves? Was it not people of colour who first studied the constellations and predicted the motion of the stars? Science and technology is in our genes, it is our birthright and, unless we master it, we'll enter the 21st century by dancing right back into slavery.

1966: Black Panther Party formed in Oakland, California, by Huey P. Newton and Bobby Seale.

We must learn to lean upon ourselves.

April 11

When I think of the 10-year-old orphans in Somalia, shining shoes for pennies to feed their younger siblings, I want to do something about it. I can. You see, my problems are like pleasures in comparison.

1789: Black musical prodigy George P. Bridgtooer, performs in Paris to rave reviews.

Better look out, sister, how you walk on de cross Yo' foot might slip and yo' soul git lost
Negro spiritual

April 12

1855: James W.C. Pennington successfully sues a New York horse-car company after being forcibly removed.

Treat all men alike. Give them all the same law. Give them all an even chance to live and grow. All men were made by the same Great Spirit Chief. They are all brothers. The earth is the mother of all people, and all people should have equal rights upon it. You might as well expect the rivers to run backward as expect that a man who was born free should be contented when penned up and denied liberty to go where he pleases.

Chief Joseph

My African forefathers taught me the right way. I shall live by their example.

April 13

1990: Neville Clare, Jamaica; Irma Critchlow, London; Linbert Spencer, Luton and Sam Selvon, Trinidad & Tobago, each receive a *Caribbean Times* award for their work in the community.

Dream Variation
To fling my arms wide
In some place of the sun,
To whirl and to dance
Till the white day is done.
Then rest at cool evening
Beneath a tall tree
While night comes on gently,
    Dark like me—
                    Langston Hughes

Accept your place in the sun.
Elijah Mohammad

April 14

Nothing under heaven is softer or more yielding than water, but when it attacks things hard and resistant there is not one of them that can prevail. For they can find no way of altering it. That the yielding conquers the resistant and the soft conquers the hard is a fact known by all men, yet utilised by none... What is of all things most yielding can overwhelm that which is of all things most hard. Being without substance it can enter even where there is no space. That is how I know the value of action that is actionless. But that there can be teaching without words. Value in action that is actionless. Few indeed can understand.

The Way and its Power.

1996: Government leaders from all 53 African countries sign treaty to outlaw nuclear weapons.

I am sick and tired of being sick and tired.

April 15

I am an optimist, not just because I have a positive view of life, but because there is so much about me that promises great achievement and that is a continual source of stability and strength. I am even willing to fail many times, if need be, if I can accomplish a little good. My quest for greatness is what makes me get up early to jog a circuit and prepare myself properly for the day to come. And when you see me taking great care in choosing what I eat, it is because I have come to understand that to poison your body is to poison your mind and ultimately to poison your soul. That road never leads to success.

1894: Chattanooga, Tennessee. Bessie Smith, 'Empress of the blues' born.

People see God every day, they just don't recognise him.
Pearl Bailey

April 16

1943: All black _Carmen Jones_ appears on Broadway. A first for African-America.

The HAPPINESS you long for is within the best of your ability. It's not easy trying to do your best. It's easier to do just enough or to stand on the corner skylarking. You'll always have to pay in the end for your lack of effort. There is no mercy for those who have ability and waste it. Go the extra mile today and your reward will be HAPPINESS.

Material deprivation is horrible, but it does not compare to spiritual deprivation.
Martin Delany

April 17

1984: David Dabydeen wins the Commonwealth Prize for poetry with _Slave Song_, written in Creole.

True success is measured not by the position you have reached in life, but by the obstacles which you have overcome while trying to succeed. The greater the obstacles the more impressive the success. Think of the obstacles people of colour have conquered in the last hundred years and you will understand how truly great we are. However, today many of us view these obstacles as stumbling blocks and give up too easily when we meet them. Let these obstacles spur you on to greater things — to reach your full potential.

I am what time, circumstance, history, have made of me, certainly, but I am also much more than that. So are we all.
James Baldwin

April 18

How much poorer we would be if we chose not to mix with other peoples? Let us not isolate ourselves from other cultures. Instead, we should dip into them and see what positive we can find. True, BLACK IS BEAUTIFUL, but there's nothing wrong with enjoying Mediterranean cooking or learning Japanese. Being BLACK AND BEAUTIFUL is only a part of the bigger picture. You'll find something positive in every corner of the human community.

1960: Harry Belafonte becomes first black entertainer to win an Emmy Award for his TV show, *Tonight with Harry Belafonte.*

We do not want a Nation, we are a Nation . . . We are a people. We are unconscious captives unless we realise this.
Amiri Baraka

April 19

Some of us like to blame 'the man' for holding us back. But the truth is much closer to home. How often do we take an active role in government elections, local or national? Do we even know who our elected officers are, or our union representative at work? Do we encourage our children to become politicians or politically active? If we ourselves do not take a deep and vigorous interest in the issues that affect our daily lives and are not prepared to make an effort on our own behalf, how can we expect those that are our elected officers to bother? We must not sit back and allow others to dictate our lives. If we do not shout at the top of our voices, our silence will be taken as consent.

1976: Barbara Jordan, makes keynote speech at the US Democratic Convention. A first for Black America.

I asked myself, Where is the black man's government? Where is his president, his country, and his ambassador, his army, his navy, his men of big affairs? I could not find them, and then I declared, "I will help to make them."
Marcus Garvey

April 20

The most important challenge in my life is to always test the limits of my abilities, do the best job I can at the time while remaining true to myself.

April 21

Like you, I am on a journey to selfhood, the gradual appreciation of myself as a unique individual. I have learned to distinguish between the facts and the truth of my life story and to carefully select those events in my life that helped me to grow emotionally, psychologically and spiritually. This is the "stuff of life" that truly counts in building ME. Throughout my journey, I have been amazed at the strength of my sistas and their ability to prevail despite the hurt put upon them in the world. Think what we could achieve if we worked together. On second thoughts, let's not think about it, let's just DO IT!

April 22

Every generation must learn of the many great deeds and achievements of black heroes and heroines in the hall of fame. Too numerous to mention — the many medical discoveries that have alleviated suffering and given billions of people a better quality of life, the engineering advances which ensure that we have safe vehicles, roads and homes and the arts in which we excel above all others, are the cornerstones of our inspiration. When, as children, we learn of these triumphs we wish to emulate them. Remember how many of us wanted to sing like The Jackson 5 or fight like Muhammed Ali? But we were never taught about the achievements of Toussaint L'Ouverture, Shaka, Nanny, Harriet Tubman, Sojourner Truth. If we had been taught about them, maybe we would emulate them also.

1978: Ghetto leaders Bucky Marshall and Claudie Massop unite to halt Jamaica's black on black violence with a One Love Peace Concert in Kingston.

You command your own destiny and that destiny can eventually embrace the stars.

April 23

Ignorant people will try and make us feel ashamed of our past, our history. The negative responses we get from others make us feel we do not belong. At these times we should look back to where we came from and revel in our ancestors' great civilisations. You are of nobler and more respectable birth than the Queen of England. She should bow down to you! So what could anyone possibly say that would make you ashamed of what and who you are? Read your history, because the past is a beacon to show us the way in the future, for ourselves and coming generations. We are a rich diaspora and we have every reason to hold our heads high with grace and dignity.

1872: Charlotte E. Ray gains her Law degree from Howard University, becoming America's first black female Law graduate.

History, despite its wrenching pain, cannot be unlived, but if faced with courage, need not be lived again.
Maya Angelou

April 24

1868: African-American Edmonia Lewis, self-taught sculptress, completes *Forever Free*, celebrating the Emancipation Proclamation.

Why do we suffer so much abuse, so much disrespect and heartache? Why are we left abandoned with two kids on the floor and another one on its way? Why do we have to fend for ourselves? Why do we have to learn to protect ourselves and our loved ones? Why do we have to learn to be mother AND father? Because they don't make brothas like they used to.

Each one teach one.

April 25

1991: Forbes publishes list of richest U.S. entertainers: Bill Cosby ($113 million), Oprah Winfrey ($80 million), Michael Jackson ($60 million).

I don't think you heard me the first time, so I'll say it again: The revolution will NOT be televised, The revolution will be LIVE!

A sense of one's self in the world is a good thing. Not to be confused with selfishness. Selfishness thinks only of its own importance. With a true sense of self you will see yourself in relation to others. The time for the "ME" generation has past, the "WE" generation is taking over. It's a whole new world, a dazzling place with a fantastic new point of view. Surround yourself with people who know their worth and that of everyone around them.

April 26

A king ordered his chief counsellor, "Bring me the sweetest food on land or sea!" The chief counsellor came back with a tongue on a platter, cooked with fine herbs and spices. After eating it, the king commanded: "Bring me the most bitter food known to man." The chief counsellor went away and, again, he brought a tongue. The king was confused and angry. "I asked you to bring me something sweet and you gave me a tongue, then I asked for something bitter and, again, you bring me a tongue." The chief counsellor replied: "Yes, oh great King, there is nothing in all the world sweeter than a tongue and nothing more bitter."

1788: William Cuffay, one of the principal leaders of the Chartist movement, the first mass political movement for the black British working classes.

I am overwhelmed by the grace and persistence of my people.
Maya Angelou

April 27

Once, long ago, there were two men who lived in a great city. One was constantly in tears and the other was always laughing. The first man was asked: "Good things and bad, funny things and sad — why do you weep through all of them?" The man replied: "What else can I do? Our lives are short, all mankind indulges in the pleasures of this life and has no mind for the eternal. I weep for all who are preparing purgatory for themselves." The second man was asked why he was always so cheerful. "Life is fleeting," he replied, "all men are drawn towards evil and do nothing good. I have tried to point them in the right direction, but no one listened to me. So now I can only laugh... What good will it do to them or to myself, if I give way to despair on their account?"

1960s: Singer Shirley Bassey becomes the first black entertainer to have her own show on British national television.

He who hopes fares better than he who wishes, and he who wishes fares better than he who disappears.
Moroccan proverb

April 28

1975: Arthur Ashe becomes the first black man to win the Wimbledon tennis championship and by so doing inspires countless young African-American tennis hopefuls.

The most important thing that we can learn to do today is think for ourselves ... When you come to make a decision, you have to weigh all of what you've heard on its own, and place it where it belongs, and come to a decision for yourself; you'll never regret it. It is very important to think out a situation for yourself. If you don't do it, you'll always be manoeuvred into a situation where you are never fighting your actual enemies, where you will find yourself fighting your own self.

Malcolm X

You are the sum total of your thoughts.

April 29

1957: Sir Edward Okyere Asafu-Adjaye, the first Asante lawyer and the first Ghanaian High Commissioner to the UK after independence.

Put thirty spokes together and we call it a wheel. But the strength of the wheel depends on the empty spaces between the spokes. In the same way that we take advantage of what is, we should also recognise the usefulness of what isn't. Consider what isn't in your life and you will be immediately stronger for having done so.

Don't feel entitled to anything you haven't worked hard for.

April 30

For the sake of advancement, we must learn to transcend the wrongs that have been done, the suffering which has been caused to us, our parents and our great-grandparents, and allow the scars to heal, both physically and mentally. Yes, fight injustice and oppression wherever you find them, but you must also move on. The universe will right all wrongs in its own way and time. Feeling embittered and maligned will not bring about the justice you seek any quicker. Meanwhile, you have things to do, people to meet, places to visit.

1995: Connie Marks, 70, (came to the UK from Jamaica in the 1950s), battles singlehandedly to ensure that black heroine Mary Seacole's house in central London becomes a national monument.

You should be building bridges, not walls.

May 1

I am a woman who came from the cotton fields of the South. I was promoted from there to the washtub. Then I was promoted to the cook kitchen, and from there I PROMOTED MYSELF into the business of manufacturing hair goods and preparations... I have built my own factory on my own ground. *Madame C.J. Walker*

1890: African-American William B. Purvis granted patent for the fountain pen.

The breaking day has wisdom, the falling day, experience. **Nadangan proverb.**

May 2

1997: Controversial African-American academic Professor Patricia Williams, becomes the first black woman to deliver the BBC's prestigious Reith Lectures in London.

For news of the heart, ask the face.
Hausa proverb

Have we forgotten the contribution that people of colour have made to the spheres of the arts, from sculpture to modern dance? Our neglect of this aspect of our heritage, limits the scope of our lives. Tap into the energy source of the ancient artisans. Discover their talents and enrich yours.

May 3

1981: US Air Force abandons policy of discrimination against people with a genetic predisposition to Sickle Cell Anaemia.

The fool is thirsty in the midst of water.
Ethiopian Galla

We wear the mask that grins and lies,
It hides our cheeks and shades our eyes,
This debt we pay to human guile;
With torn and bleeding hearts we smile.
But let the world dream otherwise,
We wear the mask.

Paul Laurence Dunbar

May 4

I have learned to enjoy the unpredictability of conversation. I like its immediacy... the mistakes... the insights... the risks inherent in hot discussion, the wisdom that can be gained through 'reasoning'. Life is all about the balance between risk and inertia... a poetic equation.

1992: With the publication of his first novel, *Yardie*, novelist Victor Headley triggers the 'Brixton rennaissance' of black British writing, with 100s of other black writers following in his footsteps. *Take life. It's yours, God give it to you free. It's as free as the air you breathe.* **Nubia Kai**

May 5

I will not allow one prejudiced person or one hundred million to blight my life. I will not let prejudice or any of its humiliations and injustices bear me down to spiritual defeat. My inner life is mine and I shall maintain its integrity against all the powers of hell.
James Weldon Johnson

1838: Mary Ann Shadd edits and publishes *The Provisional Freeman*, a paper for fugitive slaves in Canada. The motto is "Self-reliance is the true road to independence".

Let no one and nothing have your soul.

May 6

1800s: James Horton, a black medical student in Edinburgh University, is appointed to the British army as a medical officer.

Proceed, great chief, with virtue on thy side,
Thy ev'ry action let the goddess guide.
Phillis Wheatley

Behold, I bring you good news of great joy and glad tidings. Though you are created of the dust of the earth, God has also breathed the breath of a spiritual life into your nostrils and you have become living souls. You are ashamed because you are black. But I tell you, God Almighty estimates a man by the worth of his soul and not the colour of his skin. When the angel troubles the pool, you are waiting for some friend to lift and carry you into the healing waters. But I say unto you, as Christ said unto the man sick of the palsy, "Rise, take up thy bed and walk". Make a supreme effort to rise and get into the pool yourself and you will command the respect and challenge the admiration of a hostile world. You can operate factories, found cities and build up enterprises the same as other men.

Marcus Garvey

May 7

1939-45: Over 80,000 black men and women gave their services to Britain in World War II.

Read stories to your children with heroes and heroines who look just like them.

When they learn the fairy tales of mythical kings, we must let them hear of the Pharaohs and African kings. Caesar? We must teach them of Hannibal and his Africans. Shakespeare? We must teach them of Pushkin and Dumas. Whatever the white man has done, we have done, often better.

Mary McLeod Bethune

May 8

When you begin a great work you can't expect to finish it all at once...press on, and let nothing discourage you till you have entirely finished what you have begun. The contrary winds may blow strong, go forward and never turn back, and continue to press forward until you have finished. Though you may hear birds singing on this side and that side, you must not take notice of that...

Teedyuscung Delaware

1922: Hazel Harrison, pianist, debuts in New York City playing classical music composed by black people.

Hope is the pillar of the world.
Kanuri proverb

May 9

Your house is a reflection of who and what you are, the level of consciousness you have attained. If your house is in order, neat and well kept, you are content and at peace within the temple of your soul. However, if chaos rules, that is the sign of internal confusion, conflict and unrest. Your home is a refuge from the world, a sacred place, a place to gain composure and peace. Remove the items that merely add to the clutter, and have no use. Prepare yourself for the coming day. Make your home a place where you recharge your spiritual batteries before going out into the world.

1887: Taytu Betul, empress of Ethiopia, personally financed the first hotel in Addis Ababa.

Confidence, conviction and action will cause us to be free men today.
Marcus Garvey

May 10

1958: Sidney Poitier nominated for an Oscar as best actor for his role in *The Defiant Ones*.

People of colour, why do we fight amongst ourselves? Why do we quarrel? We are the embodiment of grace, dignity and majesty. We manifest the highest principles of mind, body, spirit, thought, word and deed. We are brothers and sisters in spirit. Why do we mistreat each other? What hurts one hurts the whole. Together we must turn our environment into a paradise of peace to enhance our souls. Each one of us is special. Each one of us is precious. Each one of us is sacred.

Lift up yourselves... Take yourselves out of the mire and hitch your hopes to the stars.
Marcus Garvey

May 11

1934: African-American Thomas A. Dorsey establishes the first gospel publishing company, Dorsey House.

Black, brown, golden. We are truly people of colour. Though diverse in experience, desires, of beauty, we share one ancestor. It's in the reflection in our eyes and the love we radiate. It's in our smile and the way we relate to each other. It's in our beauty. Black beauty, brown beauty. The fullness of our lips and the curves of our hips are the wealth of that great civilisation to which we belong. People of colour, rise up and take your crown. Let others worship and pay homage at your shrine.

Unity comes about by love, truth and good purpose.

May 12

We must learn to remove the antagonism that exists between us. We must exchange love. Let it inspire, strengthen and nurture us. Let it go on forever, unconditionally. Let love exist in your children, so that they are beautiful in spirit and know that they are special. Let love teach you the lessons of life and give you the tools with which you will survive and prosper. Let it cleanse you and remove all negative thoughts about yourself and others. May love give you fortitude to overcome adversity. Let it bring you together as one.

1974: Beverly Johnson becomes one of the top high fashion models, and appears on the cover of *Vogue*. A first for an African-American model.

No colour comes after black.
Proverb

May 13

The girls and women of our race must not be afraid to take hold of business endeavours. I started in business with one dollar and fifty cents. I went on to employ more than a thousand women... I have made it possible for many women of colour to abandon the washtub for a more pleasant and profitable occupation.

Madam C.J. Walker

1926: Paul R. Williams becomes the first African-American man to become a member of the American Institute of Architects.

Been in sorrow's kitchen and licked out all the pots.

May 14

Pessimists have nothing better to do than share their dour outlook with you. Pay them no heed. They want you to give up as they have done. Keep Cool. No need to fret more than you did yesterday. Keep Cool. When you started healing you threw out all negative thought out of the window. You have every reason to be optimistic about your life, as is evident from that smile that's been on your face since the process began. Nothing can stop you now, least of all the negative thinking of a pessimist. KEEP COOL!!

Africans unite! Recycle the black dollar.

May 15

Acknowledge where you have come from, from whom you have descended. Pay homage to those who have gone before, who have enabled you to progress this far. Strong black men and women, good and true. Those with a spirit strong enough to break boundaries and make sacrifices for the benefit of those who follow. Always remember to thank your parents for what they have done for you, and honour them for facilitating your passage through life.

Search your mother's face and see how much of yourself you owe this woman.

May 16

Life/personality must be taken as a total entity. All of your life is all of your life and no one incident stands alone, no situation can be obliterated. Every piece contributes to the completion of the puzzle, even those negative pieces you were responsible for.

1891- 1962: Manan Janterar Asfaw, wife of Ethiopian Emperor Haile Selassie, believed passionately in education for girls and built a girl's college with her own money. She also founded the Ethiopian Women's Association.

In God we trust, all others cash.

May 17

Discipline is the first prerequisite for learning. You can read all the books in the world and go to the best schools, but without discipline you will learn little or nothing. How can you teach your children without discipline? How can you learn yourself without discipline?

1997: The market for black hair care and cosmetic products in Britain today, is worth over £30million a year, much of which is generated by black British companies.

When you kill the ancestor, you kill yourself.
Toni Morrison

May 18

1996: Black athlete Tessa Sanderson takes part in her fourth Olympics in a row. A record for a British female.

You can't really make much of a difference in things until you change yourself.
Alice Walker

Often we feel disheartened when we see decay and lawlessness surrounds us. We feel incensed yet powerless to help. WE ARE THE WORLD. We may not be able to save the planet, but by making little changes in our own lives we can begin to make the world a better place. The troubles and pain of the world are your troubles and pain. The rain that nourishes the earth, nourishes you too. One world. One love. One destiny.

May 19

1925: Malcolm X born. His life will touch the lives of every black man, woman and child in America and throughout the diaspora. He gave his life for his people.

A smile is a light in the window of your face that shows your heart is at home.
African proverb

Start your day early with some quiet time. Time to meditate. It doesn't have to be deep meditation, just enough peaceful space to centre yourself to face the day ahead. Try to tap into that spiritual side of yourself. If you go out without that intact, your day will be confused, incomplete, unfulfilled.

May 20

We have slipped into a cultural stupor, we have forgotten the great oral traditions of our ancestors and allowed the exploits of our heroes and heroines to remain unsung. Who will remember how great Harriet Tubman was if we don't keep reminding them? Who will give Aretha Franklin 'respect' if we don't. Their greatness should not be forgotten. We must document their triumphs and tribulations, before someone else writes our history for us. We must dream our dreams, put them out in words and conserve them for posterity in books. Make your home a library of your deeds so that we can all share in its rich diversity.

1864: The first novel written by a slave is published. *The President's Daughter* by William Wells Brown.

A novel is something you have to reflect on; you have to dream about it. Black women do not have time to dream.
Miriam Tlali

May 21

My family on my mother's side are survivors. My family on my father's side are fighters. I am a revolutionary. It is only logical.

1996: Diran Adebayo becomes the first male author to be published by UK feminist publishers Virago with his debut novel *Some Kind Of Black*, which wins the Writer's Guild's 'New Author' award.

Say it loud: I am young, gifted and black.

May 22

1800s: African descendant Frances Batty Shand, founds the Association for Improving the Social and Work Conditions for the Blind of Cardiff, Wales.

Even in the worst situations, you still have the choice between the high road and the low road. Rudolph Fisher.

Woman

Wife, mother, daughter, sister, friend. These are the roles we assigned to you.
Love, care, compassion, trust, suppliant, reserved are the emotions we allow you to have.
You are much more than these names or roles that are put upon you like the garment you wear.

WOMAN — your name is not Wife alone.
WOMAN — your name is not Mother alone.
WOMAN — your name is not Daughter alone.
WOMAN — your name is not Sister alone.
WOMAN —
You are whatever you want to be. Labelled or free, the choice is yours. Define your name yourself and fulfil your destiny.

May 23

1996: Lee Jasper launches Operation Black Vote in London arguing that we CAN change things.

Imagine the impact if one million black people called up the prime minister today...

Man

Husband, father, son, brother, friend.
Strong, aggressive, hunter, gatherer, leader, enforcer — these are the emotions we allow you to have. You are much more than these names or roles that you wear like the latest fashion.

MAN — your name is not husband but love.
MAN — your name is not father but joy.
MAN — your name is not son but peace.
MAN — your name is not friend but charity.
MAN —
You are whatever you want to be, the choice is yours. Define your name yourself and fulfil your own destiny.

May 24

The values of our ancestors have been lost through the passing of time and the break-up of our extended families. It is hard to define and maintain a sense of our heritage when we are surrounded by alien culture. Sometimes all we are left with is our personal integrity to guide us through life.

1978: Viv Anderson became the first black player to be picked for England's national soccer team.

Take an honest assessment of what you do and do not like about yourself, and evaluate how much of your feelings are based on white beauty standards or symbols of success.
Evelyn C.White

May 25

Women of colour have long been at odds with themselves. A bitter war of attrition has been waged in the bathrooms and salons across the diaspora. Before your next trip to the salon to straighten your hair, pause and think, "Are these alterations made in order to make me feel happier with myself or is it a way of conforming to totally alien standards of beauty?" Find the love within and set yourself free.

1997: African Liberation Day. The universally agreed day when rejoicing African people, throughout the diaspora, give thanks and praises.

Be loyal to yourselves: your skin, your hair, your lips your laughing kindness.
Ossie Davis

May 26

1997: Olympic sprint medallist Ato Boldon puts his money where his mouth is, by setting up Athletes Towards the Olympics, a fund to help young athletes in his home country Trinidad.

No one can figure out your worth but you.

The problem seems daunting, but the solution is so simple a child could solve it. Yet, we can't see it, so we call on all our intellectual faculties to assist us. The greatest problems of life are solved by babies every day. We learned to feed by instinct and desire. When we learned to walk, we placed one foot in front of the other which led us to the right solution. If we adults took what we learned as children we would not struggle to do somersaults when a few careful steps are all that is needed. What was hidden from the wise, is now revealed to the babes and suckling.

May 27

1987: Brenda Edwards becomes the first black female member of the London Festival Ballet Company.

I really don't think life is about the I-could-have-beens. . . Life is only about the I-tried-to-do. I don't mind the failure but I can't imagine that I'd forgive myself if I didn't try.
Nikki Giovanni

We are the product of a process which initially took nine months. As we grow the process continues: learning, discovering, experimenting. Trial and error is part of the process. When we fall in love and out of it, still we are part of a process. When we hate and learn to forgive we evolve by a process. The mourning of a loved one and the stages of bereavement are part of the healing process. As the cells of our body develop, mature and die, we live a process. Each stage is vital, not to be missed, forgotten or overlooked. When we learn from our mistakes, build on our success and continuously evolve we are part of the process. When we give up, give in or shut down we are liable to be run over by the process!

May 28

Personal achievement is my goal. I used to come last, but I work hard. I practice regularly, I persevere and, with my talents slowly emerging, I am succeeding bit by bit.

1976: Pearl Connor changed the face of classical music with her jazz improvisation of Bach, broadcast on the BBC.

Listen to your soul - the voice of your ancestors urging you to 'do the right thing'.

May 29

What's in a name? Plenty! They can hurt us, reduce us, devalue us, and prevent our growth. If negative names, tags and labels can reek this much havoc, just think of all the good that positive, loving, uplifting, affirming names can do.

1939-45: Dr. Ernest Goffe, a Jamaican doctor in St Ann's Hospital, Tottenham, London, treats bomb victims of World War II.

I wanted a name associated with the liberation of our people. Assata means 'She who struggles', Shakur means 'the thankful'.
Assata Shakur

May 30

1990: Seven top black UK actors, fed up of waiting for their agents to call, decide to produce their own shows as The Posse. They become hugely successful.

We cannot do good when the original thought was steeped in malice. We cannot be even-handed with everyone when we have in us a grain of prejudice. We cannot be powerful when our wish is to oppress. We cannot show appreciation when we consider nothing of value. We cannot be generous with our time, ourselves, money, if we do not think that what we have is enough for us to share with others. We cannot exhibit our talents if we do not appreciate our diversity and uniqueness.

The heart can not hold two.
Egyptian proverb

May 31

1982: Mrs Kallon beats seven male candidates to become the first woman to be elected to the Sierra Leone parliament.

When you have thought of who you want to be, what you want to do, then be it and do it. What is the good of thought without action? Until you DO, you are only half the person you could be.

He who gives you the diameter of your knowledge, prescribes the circumference of your activity.
Minister Louis Farrakhan

June 1

You will have heard people say: "As a woman you can't know anything about cars and engines." "As a man you should not like staying at home, looking after the children." "You are old, act your age." "You are black, you can't like or understand classical music." Shouldn'ts, cants, not allowed tos, not supposed to be, are the harnesses that people like to place on us, when we want to go our own way. If we listen to them long enough we are in danger of being the stereotype that these phrases make for us. If we quietly accept them we will become entrapped by them. Our ability cannot be restricted by our race, gender or creed. The Creator embraces diversity. What a dull and unattractive world it would be otherwise.

1977: *Roots* the mini series, outdoes *Gone With The Wind* when 130 million watch it on television.

We will either find a way or make one.
Hannibal

June 2

You are free when you allow your thoughts to be. You are free when you are satisfied by your own efforts. You are free when you set targets for yourself to reach goals in the future. You are free when you can say "no" to this and "yes" to that. You are free when you choose the people you want to be with. You are free when you choose to be alone. If you are unsatisfied with your life, achieving nothing that you value, accepting nothing and rejecting everything and are surrounded by worthless people, you are not free. Examine your mind, life, and the people around you then ask yourself if you are free.

1994: *Baby Father* becomes London's fastest selling black book. "People used to say if you want to hide something from a black man, put it in a book," says author Patrick Augustus.

It is only what is written upon the soul of man that will survive the wreck of time.
Francis J Grimke.

June 3

As a child, sometimes there was not enough food at home to make a complete meal or the right clothes in the wardrobe to wear a matching outfit. But I never fell prey to the despair of the streets around me, because I inherited an old-fashioned decency from my mother, that encompassed a host of values such as modesty, faith and perseverance. In this bitter, cynical world, such old-fashioned values are still turning out great doctors and lawyers.

If you want to accomplish the goals of your life, you have to begin with the spirit.
Oprah Winfrey

June 4

Take this and it will give you bright eyes, shiny hair and radiant skin. Have this and your job will improve and your boss will notice you. Do this every day and your friends will admire you and be drawn to you. What is it that you need to take, have or do? Not a patent pill or potion, not a weave, new gadget or tool, or a new form of exercise. But love, self-esteem, empowerment and self-reward.

Silence is deafening to one who listens hungrily.

June 5

When we take care of US we nurture ourselves. Take the trouble to find out what you REALLY need, what is REALLY good for you and what REALLY rocks your world. Take pride in yourself and in your work, whatever you choose to do, do it well. You do not have to turn to technology to produce a modern alternative to nurturing. You already have the oldest trick, the original recipe in the book — LOVE!

1993: Paul Ince becomes the first black player to captain the English national soccer team.

Whatever I wanna do and be Mother, Father, God already gave it to me.
Queen Afua.

June 6

You are not run-of-the-mill, humdrum, mediocre, one of the masses, part of the furniture. If only we could see our own "star quality", we would not settle for second best. If we could see how remarkable our talents are, we would not remain in jobs that did not use our talents and gifts. If we could see the amount of love we are capable of giving and receiving we would not stay in relationships that deplete our energy, unbalance our equilibrium and reduce our sense of self. If we could see what we are worth, we would demand the highest and best treatment and quality of life for ourselves. When we see ourselves in the light of the Creator we will no longer tremble.

1942: Clarinettist Rudolf Dunbar, makes his conducting debut with the London Philharmonic Orchestra at the Royal Albert Hall.

Being distracted by shading or colouring of skin is stupid. It gets in the way.
Ray Charles

June 7

1940s: Dr. Goffe Jr., a second generation Jamaican in Britain, was part of the team who formulated the polio vaccine.

May your heart ever be full of the love of loving.

Nourish your family with a loving, creative and moral atmosphere. Eat meals together as often as you can and use the opportunity to promote positive images and take pride in each other's accomplishments. There is little to remind us daily of how powerful and capable we are, so we must do that for ourselves and each other.

June 8

1921: *Shuffle Along*, a collaboration of pianist and composer Eubie Blake, and singer Nobel Sissle, opens in New York City, runs for 504 performances and tours for another two years.

You are what your dreams are.
Benjamin Mays

The world is full of stereotypes. Do you listen to the ones that tell you that you are from a proud nation, versed in poetry, literature and the arts? Do you see the signs of your heritage in the buildings and governments that surround you? Do you hear the pounding beat, and lyrics that tell of great battles, wise and noble deeds and families connected and motivated by the well being of all? Have you seen the images of wealth, modernity, and are influenced by the beliefs that all aid the upliftment of the race? There are people who would place us in pigeon holes and mark us with racial stereotypes. But when we look at the truth it leads to a vast heritage that stretches back to the beginning of time. I refuse to be stereotyped, unless you wish to stereotype me as a typical successful black woman.

June 9

As you watch TV or listen to the radio you cannot help but be bombarded by the wealth of black talent out there. Actors on stage, film and theatre, dancers and playwrights. Young bands, painters, sculptors. We are without question a nation and people who were born creative. We take our hair and make it into an art form, we wear our clothes this way and everyone follows, we lift our voices and sing the sweetest bitter-sweet songs. We ooze with eloquent expression. EXPRESS YOURSELF.

1872: African-American Elijah McCoy patents the first automatic lubricator supplying oil to moving parts of an engine, and inspires the term 'the real McCoy'.

I've known rivers ancient as the world and older than the flow of human blood in human veins.
Langston Hughes

June 10

You have read the book, seen the film, bought the T-shirt, seen the sculptures, been to the concerts, can talk the talk and copy the stance. But do you really know what it is to be black? You have read *his* story and *her* version, but do you know how your family got its name, or came to be where they are now? You have seen *his* film, *their* adaptation, but when are you going to write your script and cast yourself in the lead role? Until we know what blackness truly means all we are doing is buying into the experience. Blackness comes from knowledge of our heritage and living through it as its descendants. So, will the REAL BLACK PEOPLE please stand up.

1840s: Slave Dred Scott takes his owners to court to free himself and his family. He hires a lawyer for $300.

Happy the sons whom fathers educate.

June 11

1933: African-American composer Florence Price's symphony is performed by the Chicago Symphony Orchestra.

The colour of the skin is in no way connected with strength of the mind or intellectual powers.
Benjamin Banneker

When we have men who can impart to their sons a sense of what it is to be a "real man", then the race is strengthened. When we have sons who have gained distance for themselves yet are umbilically linked to their fathers, then the race will move forward. When we have men who hero worship their fathers yet see their clay feet, then the race cannot falter. When we have men who can think for themselves yet are humble enough to receive wise counsel, then the race is truly blessed. When we have men who are as courageous in their intimacy as they are in their pursuits, then indeed we have a loving race.

June 12

1991: Ms Elaine Foster becomes the first black female headmistress of a secondary school in Birmingham, England.

The world is before you and you need not take it or leave it as it was when you came in.
James Baldwin

I am here, in the here and now. I will deal with the here and now. I know my past and how it affects me in the here and now. I have my future which flows from the here and now. I will make my choices, here and now based on my past and my here and now. My dreams may be of the future but they start in the here and now. I can taste, feel, touch today, so that when tomorrow becomes the here and now I will have the memory of today and use it to make a better here and now.

June 13

Our generation have rights which have been won for us by those who have gone before. The right to vote as women, and people of colour. The right to determine our future as individuals and as a nation. The freedom to choose what we watch or read. The freedom to live where we like. When we neglect our responsibilities, we belittle the effort that others have made on our behalf. We now take these fundamental human rights for granted. But if we are to pass on to future generations their rightful legacy, we must protect our freedom that has been fought for so valiantly.

1979: Arthur Lewis becomes the first black economics professor in Britain and wins the Nobel Prize for Economics.

Words set things in motion.
Toni Cade Bambara

June 14

When we are single-minded in our demands our voice will be heard. When our hearts beat as one, then we truly shall overcome — someday! That day is here, and the time is now!

1988: Lawyers Leonard Woodley & John Roberts, become the first black QCs to take silk in Britain.

When spider webs unite, they can tie up a lion.
African proverb

June 15

1970: Chief Ralph Uwechue launches *Africa* magazine and *African Woman* in 1975, then in 1991, *Know Africa Books*, *Africa Today*, *Africa Who's Who* and *The Makers of Modern Africa*.

Meditation is not a substitute for having money in the bank or the fragrance of a rose. Meditation cannot replace a warm embrace and true love. But it does enhance those experiences when we have them, and it keeps us aware of the lasting happiness within when we don't. Discover your source of inner happiness, it is more lasting than the 'happiness' of the world outside.

It's a Black thang, I KNOW you understand it.

June 16

1866-68: Tewodros II reunified the Ethiopian empire and was the first emperor to seek modernisation of the country.

PLAY, something so fundamental that teaches us co-ordination, communication skills, co-operation, self-sufficiency, stamina and flexibility. We couldn't pay for a course that could teach us so many skills that are necessary for life, and we got it free, without knowing it. PLAY. The games we played as children prepared us for adulthood. Remember doctors and nurses! When we no longer play, we lose our childish inquisitiveness and uninhibited joy. If we could only find the time to take the business of play seriously as infants do, we would learn so much about life.

Do a common thing in an uncommon way.
Booker T. Washington

June 17

When our parents taught us that we must always stand tall, look sharp and step lively, the lesson was twofold. In a day and time where first impressions count for so much, we are rarely allowed a second chance in which to show our best side. When we step out we have to look as if we mean business, are on a mission, and look people squarely in the eye. Also, when we stand tall we take up space, being ignored is impossible. When you catch yourself slouching, pull yourself up, draw in your stomach, look straight ahead and remind yourself of your determination to make an impression in life.

1996: Uganda and Tanzania gain Stock Exchanges.

Your children need your presence more than your presents.
Jesse Jackson

June 18

My life will light up if my mind does. The quality of our lives are enhanced, not so much by acquiring more wealth and status, but by investing our minds with quality thoughts.

1921: James Pride Johnson records the first jazz piano solo, *The Harlem Strut*, in New York City.

The best time to do a thing, is when it can be done.
William Pickens

June 19

1996: Mark Hendrick is the only black British Member of the European Parliment.

"A woman said to me the other day...
I read one of your poems about women,
I thought it very good
But it didn't say that you
        were BLACK

Now I meet you and see that you
        are BLACK
I wonder
Why you wrote the poem?

Do *they* think
we spend
our whole lives
being BLACK
for *them?*"
        Bobbi Sykes

One cannot give to a person that which he already possess.
Toussaint L'Ouverture

June 20

1892: African-American O. E. Brow receives the patent for the horseshoe.

All over the world there is an explosion of material written and presented by black people FOR black people. We are hungry to see images of ourselves in every arena — in books, magazines plays and films. Why? Because when we see a representation of ourselves in the world it gives us confidence to be who we are. When we see positive black faces in the media it confirms that we are beautiful, intelligent and capable. When we hear of black achievement we are reassured that it will, can, and has been done by us, successfully. Every book, magazine and credit that represents people of colour, inspires me, makes me smile, gives me HOPE.

Unity comes about by love, truth and good purpose.

June 21

When you judge yourself by his, hers or their standard of perfection you will never measure up. You cannot value your achievements using somebody else's currency. It is meaningless. The only standard that really matters is yours. Set your standard as high as the skies, but take care not to set them too low.

1987-8: John Barnes is the first black soccer player to be awarded the Professional Footballers Association's Player of the Year trophy.

We must use time creatively.
Martin Luther King Jr.

Know what time it is.
Public Enemy

June 22

Divas don't die. Even though some of the sistas have been worked to death. Divas don't die. Still, some of the sistas have been forced to master Solitaire.

1996: The biggest ever budget for a Channel 4 TV programme is spent to make *The Final Passage*, a two-part dramatization of Caryl Phllips' novel.

Never get weary.

June 23

1970: Cheryle Adrienne Brown becomes the first black Miss America contestant.

There is a beautiful person residing in you, and you can choose to let that beauty surface, or you can think of yourself as being unfortunately ill-equipped by nature in that department. It's down to you and your expectations of yourself.

Ef women want any rights more'n dey got, why don't dey jes' take 'em and not be talking about it?
Sojourner Truth

June 24

1906: Jack Johnson becomes the first black heavyweight champion of the world, winning 97 out of his 100 fights.

We all remember hard times, when our parents worked hard at ill-paid jobs so that we could have the opportunity of a better future. We want to give our children an even better chance than we ever had and provide them with a standard of living denied us. Some of us work so hard that we have little time to spend with our children. We try and make up our absence and allay our feelings of guilt by spending money on elaborate toys, expensive clothes and exotic trips overseas, when all we truly need to do is to be open and available for our children, flexible with our time and willing with our hearts. We may not have had computer games to play with or two holidays a year to go on as children, but we had people around us who cared and protected us. Nothing can buy the sense of security a child needs.

And the Great White Hope is still hoping...

June 25

We must not forget our history of struggle, hardship, injustice and survival. But neither can we let the past consume our lives. If we are to be successful and whole men and women in our own right, then we must transcend the pain of our lives. When we resolve the issues that have haunted us and caused damage we can begin to tackle what is happening to us in our present lives. When we take back ourself for our selves we can begin to press the grapes of wrath into a wine that is pleasing to the palate and an excellent vintage.

1972: Queen Elizabeth II awards Joycelyn Barrow the title of Dame of the British Empire, for her contribution to community relations.

Open your eyes and look within, are you satisfied with the life you're living?

June 26

Each and every day we display courage in some way. When we smile at a stranger. When we admit we are wrong. When we admit that we are hurting, ask for help and accept it. Every faltering, unsure step we make, it took courage. It takes a lot of courage to place your heart in another's hands. When you endeavour to know yourself and accept all that you are, you take the most courageous step in life. And when you listen to that still, quiet voice within you, you display the kind of courage that warriors wish they had.

1960: President Adam Osman leads Somalia to independence.

Mama exhorted her children at every opportunity to "jump at de sun". We might not land on the sun, but at least we would get off the ground. **Zora Neale Hurston**

June 27

1986: African-American Debi Thomas became the first black adult figure skating champion, winning both U.S. and world titles.

Presumption should never make us neglect that which appears easy to us.
Benjamin Banneker

Everybody needs an occasional boost in life, especially when sadness prevails. Sometimes a love light shining brightly will suffice. And sometimes a few inspirational words on a page will give us the strength to carry on. But when all else fails, I have my hands and I can pray. The burden of my troubles become so much lighter when I get down on my knees and communicate with the Almighty.

June 28

1994: Ester Mahlangu becomes the first black female artist to paint the BMW art car.

If you have no one to praise you, praise yourself.
Grebo proverb, Liberia

Assumptions can be lethal, they can kill us. When we go about thinking, "I am a mother, therefore I must always love my children whatever they do," or, "I am male therefore I must play the field," or, "I am male, I must always be strong," or, "I am black therefore everything I do, say, wear or think must be black also." Closing yourself off from other options, stunts growth and makes your horizons narrower. It prevents you from making much needed changes. We cannot change other people's assumptions of us, but we can change those we hold about ourselves. Question and challenge your assumptions and free yourself.

June 29

On the whole we are still crying, still mourning. Mourning for what was done to our parents and grandparents, for many of our national treasures which have been stolen from us, for our heroes and heroines whose exploits are left unsung. Men are crying for their loss of manhood, identity and their ability to support their families. Women are crying for the lack of support that they are receiving. We weep for the lack of unity we see around us. We are all at some stage of mourning, on one level or the other. Our tears are never futile, they are not wasted. They will lead us to ask the questions that need to be asked, and slowly start the process of healing.

1979: Elizabeth Ohene becomes the first woman to edit a national newspaper, *Graphic*, in Africa.

I find, in being black, a thing of beauty: a joy; a strength; a secret cup of gladness.
Ossie Davis

June 30

We too easily make excuses for not looking after ourselves: "I can't take time off work," "I don't want to waste the doctor's time with something silly." If we cannot make time to take care of our temples within, how can we care for and nourish our spirits?

1940: Pearl Tintou founds the National Drama Association of Trinidad & Tobago, and introduces theatre into education.

The greatest passion is compassion.
Jamaican proverb

July 1

1992: A monument commemorating the Buffalo Soldiers is commissioned by Freddie Dixon.

Being cheerful keeps you healthy. It is slow death to be gloomy all the time.
Proverbs, 17 v.22

These are RUTH-LESS times. A time where greed is held up as a virtue and comradeship means little. What we need now above all else is RUTH — mercy, compassion, love. With "ruth" we resolve the issues that divide us, appreciate others' opinions as we value our own, forgive ourselves. With "ruth", unity, peace, love and harmony are assured on a global level.

July 2

1876: African-American D.C. Fisher receives patent for furniture castor.

Walk to the beat of a different drum.

It seems like every day there's a new dance. The bogle, the running man, the butterfly, the round-the-world. Things have moved on since you last took a look. Yesterday was the funky chicken, today the funky chicken's a takeaway in south London. If you want to get with the programme, then get wise to the new dance. The old ways of doing things are out of date. The days of hustling are over. There's a new school of Young Black Entrepreneur out there and if you haven't changed also, then stay out of black business. That's the new dance. The old days of mental enslavement are over, today children of colour are demanding to be taught about their cultures and their heroes and heroines. That's the latest dance. It's an easy one. Try it and see.

July 3

If you feel that your life needs to take a different direction than that which is expected of you, then take off on your own to realise your heart's desire. It takes courage and self belief to turn your life upside down in the face of dissenting voices. Turn a deaf ear to them. Instead, listen to the music of your soul.

1980: First black public-broadcast TV station, WHMM, starts transmitting from Howard University, Washington DC.

Black is ME
Black is YOU
Black is US
Black is
BEAUTIFUL

July 4

Modern transport has caused the world to shrink. Society is so diverse that people from all over the world live next door to each other. Superficially people seem to get on. In truth our hearts and spirits are separated by huge walls which we ourselves have erected. Only when we are united in spirit can there be true peace and harmony in our communities — until then we are governed by rules. The needs of one people is much the same as another, the world is capable of providing for everyone's needs. Let us open our minds and hearts to each other, gain true understanding and nurture real love for one another. You can't pass a law that forces people to love each other. As we remain divided in heart and body we are weak; united in spirit there is no end to the great and mighty things we can accomplish.

Chief Dan George

1922: Amy Jacques marries Marcus Garvey. For years after his death in 1940, she struggled singlehandedly to keep his name and philosophy alive

My words will be a balm, not a deadly arrow.

July 5

1876: Edward Bannister's *Under the Oaks,* wins him the Centennial Exhibition in Philadelphia, the first African-American to win a major arts award.

Healing takes place within us as we speak the truth of our lives.
bell hooks

"A boy and a tiger cub were best friends until the boy became a man. One day, the young man invited his friend home. As the tiger entered, the wife exclaimed that something smelt awful. The tiger's feelings were hurt. It departed and headed for the forest. The man caught up with his friend to apologise. "Do one thing for me," the tiger said, "pick up that rock and hit me on the head." The man was horrified at the request. But after much pleading, he did as he was asked. The tiger growled with pain and ran deep into the forest. Several months later when the man was out hunting he came across his friend once again. "The wound on my head has healed, but my heart is still broken," the tiger said and walked away never to be seen again. Take care not to break somebody's heart. It may never heal.

July 6

1992: Caribbean born poet Derek Walcott wins the Nobel Prize for Literature.

You too deserve to have breakfast brought to you in bed, served on a silver tray with a single red rose in a vase. If there's no one available to do the honours, then do it yourself. You deserve it. And if you've fantasised about being driven through Paris in a sports car with the cool breeze in your hair, then now's your time to make your fantasy come true.

You can be anything you want to be...Just be the best.
David Dinkin

July 7

When we gain inner peace and happiness we touch those around us. By the way we live our lives we become an example to them, demonstrating how to behave or what to avoid. We in turn must look at others and learn from their mistakes, use their path as a guide for the route we need to take. EACH ONE REACHES OUT TO ONE!

The first black people came to Britain during the Roman Empire, over 2,000 years ago. Black communities have been living in Bristol, Liverpool and Cardiff for nearly 300 years.

Whoever wants me as I am is content.
Ghanaian proverb

July 8

Sometimes those who are closest to us do not accept the changes that we are making in ourselves and in our lives. They try to hold on to their old image and do not accept the journey we have to make. Fear of losing us motivates them, not malice. We must show them that the journey is to our mutual benefit and not their detriment. That by clinging to the old image they are preventing growth. Change in you will also force them to look at themselves. You are not the same person and, they too, will have to make a journey. This may put great stress on your relationship. Take time to show each other the way forward.

1990: Vernon Williams launches a UK appeal to collect old tools for shipment to the Caribbean to enable Jamaican youngsters to learn a trade.

Love is such a powerful force. It's there for everyone to embrace.
Coretta Scott King

July 9

1962: Professor Rex Nettleford helps establish the Jamaican National Dance Theatre Company, in a bid to " find our own voice and feet in the art of dance.

Three words which are often done to death in our society are I LOVE YOU.
I LOVE YOU — songs are sung about it.
I LOVE YOU — books are written about it.
I LOVE YOU — films illustrate it.
I LOVE YOU — on bill-boards, cards and T-shirts.
I LOVE YOU — I LOVE YOU — I LOVE YOU!
But how often do we really mean it?
When did you last say I LOVE YOU with feeling?
When did you last say it with meaning?
Said with care and tenderness I LOVE YOU is worth more than all the wealth in the world.

Dividing is to plead with death
Kigezi proverb, South-west Uganda

July 10

1987: Richard Stokes becomes the first black man to join the Royal Guards.

We cannot leave life to chance. We must prepare ourselves for every eventuality. I prepare myself for old age, by staying healthy in my body and in my mind. I do not poison my body, neither do I poison my mind. The result of either will be paid in my coming years. I prepare myself for the inevitability of death by achieving as much as I can in the short time that I am here. I no longer have time to waste, not tolerate time-wasters. I prepare my children by teaching them not to leave life to chance.

Solve your own problems by curing your own defects.

July 11

For our current relationships to work we must let go of what has gone before. We may have been hurt, disappointed and deceived, but we must try our best to put those feelings of betrayal behind us in order to let this new person who has come into our lives show us the love and tenderness they feel for us. When all we have been used to is being dumped upon and let down, we cannot believe that this new person will not treat us in the same way. Take some time to reflect on past relationships, their good and bad points, admitting where we have gone wrong and where we have hurt as much as we have been hurt. Allow time for scars to heal. Get over your hurt and set your inner house in order before embarking on a new relationship.

1996: Christopher Moori wins gold in the javelin during the Paralympics, and campaigns for recognition of disabled athletes.

There are some people that if they don't know you can't tell 'em.
Louis Armstrong

July 12

By loving yourself you automatically draw those to you who love you and wish to share their gifts with you. Believe that you deserve this love and bathe in its tranquil waters.

1952: Ralph Ellison's *Invisible Man* wins National Book Award.

Talking with one another is loving one another.
Kenyan Proverb

July 13

1790: Joshua Johnston becomes the first African-American to be recognised as a portrait painter. His work can be seen in Howard University's Gallery.

A man's bread and butter is only ensured when he works for it.
Marcus Garvey

There are times when those we love the most seem to shun every effort we make to help them. When we try to show them a different way, one that will not cause pain and difficulties, they stubbornly remain on the path that they have chosen. We must let them go. No matter how difficult it may be. All we can do is love them enough to still be there when they wake up to the truth.

July 14

1968: *Luther,* a cartoon strip by Barbara Brandon, is syndicated in U.S. newspapers, the first African-American female cartoonist to be syndicated nationally.

No matter what accomplishments you make, somebody helps you.

Remember what Mama used to say? Yet, you still went out and got yourself into trouble. You cannot protect your children from life. No matter what you do and what you say, they'll go their own way (often, the opposite direction). All you can do for them is give them a loving and stable upbringing. Then they will find their own way. But no matter which direction life blows them, that good upbringing will be right there beside them.

July 15

Do you ever get that feeling of déja vu? Like, you've been down this same old street before. You've heard these same excuses many times before and you've sworn you would never let it happen to you ever again, before. If you're serious when you say you don't want to go down this route again, then slot into place the necessary changes immediately, otherwise you'll find yourself on the same spot again, sooner than you imagined.

1990: Dame Nita Barrow becomes Barbados's first female Governor General, the culmination of an illustrious career.

A single bracelet does not jingle.
Congo proverb

July 16

Without those who laid down their lives we would not be here. Without those that have dared to defy the rules we could not have gotten so far, without those who dared to dream, our dreams could not be fulfilled. Others have laid the road so that our passage along it would be smoother. In turn we must lay further stones so that those who are to come after us may travel further still.

1992: Jacqueline Barrett becomes the first black sherriff in the U. S., when she is elected in Fulton County, Georgia.

Invite some people into your parlour and they will come into your bedroom.
Sierra Leone

July 17

1982: Martha Osamor becomes chair of Haringey Independent Police Commission, fighting for greater police accountability to the community.

Try this bracelet, if it fits wear it, but if it hurts you, throw it away no matter how shiny.
Kenyan proverb

By co-operating, so much more can be achieved. By being stubborn we insult those who wish to help us. Accept the help given to you by others, acknowledge their help on your passage through life, and do the same for those who come after you.

July 18

1990: Nelson Mandela freed after 27 years in political imprisonment. Heralds the beginning of a South Africa free of apartheid.

I need no taker to leave me half empty I'd rather be alone half full.
Nikki Grimes

Like children we rant and rage for our point of view to be accepted above others. Much more will be achieved by pooling our efforts and our ideas. Then we can go forward. Harmony does not necessarily lead to success. But with disharmony, failure is inevitable.

July 19

Gossip goes where it is not permitted. If you tell people your secrets they will discuss your affairs with others. As surely as you are discussing another's life, someone is discussing yours. The only way to prevent your intimate life from being the talk of the town is to keep it to yourself.

1992: At the age of 45, Carol Moseley-Braun becomes the first black woman elected to the U.S. senate.

Words are easy, friendship hard.
Ganda proverb (Uganda)

July 20

A great deal of our society is geared towards couples, going anywhere alone is seen as a reflection on your poor social circumstance. We feel the need to be part of the crowd; we feel that we should be in a relationship so that we can feel comfortable going to the theatre, cinema or a restaurant. Be with another if that is what you want, but be with them for the right reasons. Not because of social convention, but because of love and affection.

1984: Jesse Jackson is the first black man to run for presidential office in the U.S.

Ou okunda takushereka kigambo. (One who loves you does not spare the truth.)
Kigezi proverb

July 21

1857: Frances E.W. Harper publishes a collection of poems, selling over 10,000 copies in its first year.

The stone in the water does not know how the hill is, parched by the sun.
Nigerian proverb

We always have a choice in life, and the same applies when it comes to relationships. When they go well and both sides are benefiting we gain emotional help and joy from each other's company. But if your partner only takes while you are constantly giving, it is time to get up and get out. Take your life and heart in your hands. Decide to save yourself for someone who will give to you as much as you give them. Loneliness inside a relationship is far worse than the loneliness of being alone. Make the decision to be strong and face what you fear most rather than stay in a situation that causes pain and belittles you.

July 22

1992: *Changes,* written by Ama Ata Aidoo, wins the African section of the Commonwealth Writer's Prize.

Don't be so much in love that you can't tell when the rain comes.
Madagascan proverb

In our daily life we meet a great number of people, many of whom we only speak to for a few minutes or just smile at before we move on. Those people that we come home to, however, are the backbone of our lives, the ones we open our hearts to. These relationships require as much work as we put into our own lives. They require honesty, forgiveness and love in abundance.

July 23

Someone was hurt before you; wronged before you; hungry before you; frightened before you; raped before you; yet, someone survived.

Maya Angelou

Beware that you do not lose the substance by grasping at the shadow.
Aesop

July 24

When was the last time you had an argument? What was it about about? Money? Love? Were you in the wrong, or do you think that the other person was? When we have disagreements we are so focused on fighting our corner, proving our point, that no matter how valid the point made by the other side we will not understand them because we are not listening, we are not trying to see things from their point of view. Before the next argument arises take some time to see things from the other's point of view and in light of that make a closer examination of your own. Be strong enough to listen and loving enough to learn.

Get angry at the right things and with the right people, and in the right way and at the right time and for the right length of time.

July 25

1960: Vere C. Bird becomes Anitgua & Barbadua's first chief minister, initiating a wide range of reform in education and construction.

When we fall in love our senses are reeling, everything is exciting and our body is cooking up a cauldron of chemicals. We are so wrapped in ourselves and the object of our desire that nothing else matters. We are prone to allow other parts of our life to slip out of our grasp: work, family, friends, and ourselves. That route leads to heartache. Whilst we are "falling in love" we may slip and end up on our behinds, and then we'll need the very people we have neglected for so long. When you walk or step into love keep your eyes open, your vision clear, your footing sure and a clear memory of those who have always come to your aid in times of trouble. Don't let them suffer while you concentrate on falling in love.

Parents honour parents.
Malagasy proverb

July 26

1847: The state of Liberia is established as a homeland for former slaves returning to Africa from the Americas.

Diverse yet of one body.
My name is many and in truth
Without all parts I have no name at all.
Adjoa Andoh

In our desperate rush to be part of a couple we ignore all the aspects of the other person; we want the love and the protection but we don't want to confront the difficulties. We want the falling in love, holding hands, shared breakfast, the nice parts, the easy bits. So we overlook the truth. Illusions are the way of heartache. When I open my eyes and see a relationship for what it truly is, not for what I want it to be, then I grasp firmly on to the substance of who I am, who my partner is and what, as a pair, we can do for each other.

July 27

Anger is a wake-up call, a swift kick up the backside, an energy that crackles like electricity and galvanises you into action with its momentum, force and direction. Anger is a body with a mission. Anger breaks down barriers and rules and defies etiquette. Anger knows no shame or social taboos. Anger turns mice into lions. Anger destroys old, long-standing values and pulls new ones into play. Channeled correctly anger can be the stepping stone to building success, if you're angry enough you'll want to succeed even more. Before you lose your temper, take a deep breath in. How will you turn your anger to positive today?

1898: Mother Mary Moore, civil rights activist, born. Founder of the Black Cultural Archives in Brixton, London.

When you are rich you are hated; when you are poor, you are despised.
Ashanti proverb

July 28

Children need to know that we trust them enough to place the future in their hands. The values you instill in your children they will either take on board and hand down to their children or choose something completely different. Where else do we learn our values and attitudes from other than our homes? Give your children the tools of love, compassion and communication skills to be full and rounded adults, and you ensure that your descendants show that the line they come from is one to be admired.

1526: The first slave revolt in America. 100 Africans brought by Spanish explorer Lucas Vasquez de Ayllon, revolt after his death.

We refuse to be What you wanted us to be We are whar we are, that's the way it's going to be.
Bob Marley

July 29

1990: Cameroon becomes the first African country to reach the quarter finals of the soccer World Cup.

Of many aspirations, but one people. Diverse in colour, but one people. Strong and weak, we are one people. Through adversity, persecution and hard, hard testing. I love being black so much that, sometimes, I can hardly contain it. I want to shout it out. One people, one blood. When you strive, I strive with you. Fall and I am there to catch you. Onward and upward, one people. One body, many parts. My people are scattered, straddling the continents, our voice can be heard in every corner of the earth. When we come together in unity, we will again know our true strength. One people.

I am joy, peace, life and love, and everything else that is good.
Father Divine

July 30

1833: African-American actor Ira Aldrige plays Othello in London's Covent Garden, then Macbeth, King Lear, Shylock and Hamlet. He later performs for the kings and queens of Europe.

You have done your best. You have fulfilled your role as a partner. Now it is time for YOU to live a little. This may mean that you want to party all night long, or it may mean that you have to withdraw to that YOU within for the journey that has been calling you all along. You have done your best. You have fulfilled your role as a mother, practically on your own. It is time for someone to take the load off your back. It is time for you to be cared for, made to feel special. It is time for you to spend quality time with yourself. Enjoy. You deserve it!

Life is what YOU make of it.

July 31

If we are to make correct decisions we need as much information as we can get hold of, to evaluate the situation, and then choose the right option — EVERY TIME. Learn to develop your common sense and rely upon it. Common sense allows us to see every situation or relationship as distinct and separate and to treat it as such. Common sense is the result of careful consideration. Without it we rush headlong into crisis. Develop your common sense and use it EVERY TIME.

1995: Black newsreader Trevor McDonald, chosen to head campaign to promote better English in British schools.

Whatever I've done, I've done as well as I could and beyond.
bell hooks

August 1

When we have no self-confidence and low self-esteem we are prone to question every decision we make. We imagine that other people can give us the answers we cannot find for ourselves. Even when we do make choices we still feel the need to consult with others to gauge their opinions and give their approval. When we actively invite other people to interpret our world we give up our control and place in it. When we hold others opinions above our own, we enslave ourselves. As long as we place our lives in someone else's hands our lives will never be our own and the outcome will never make us happy. As long as we are willing to negate the role as orchestrator of our affairs, we will learn nothing about ourselves and like nothing of what we already have — knowledge.

1838: Total abolition of the slave trade in all colonies under British rule. (African slaves refused to be what they wanted them to be.)

That I exist is a perpetual surprise. But that's life.

August 2

1950-6: Alphonso E. Stennett founds and publishes *African Voice*, a magazine which gives Africans in England a forum.

Intimacy takes time. Think of all the time you spent discovering all you know about yourself, what your likes and dislikes are, what you can tolerate. All the self realisation, acceptance and eventually love for yourself — this did not just happen overnight. Similarly, in an intimate relationship, we need time to come to terms with the other person, who they are, what they stand for. Intimacy is a precious gift, which we share with ourselves and few others. Take the time to make the right connections and decisions long before you even begin to make the sexual connections.

Love begins at home, with loving yourself.
Toni Morrison

August 3

1949: African-American F.M. Jones gains patent for air conditioning unit.

Is your view of sexuality out of focus? Instead of seeing the whole person, do you zoom in on selective parts of your partner? Are you only concerned with gratification in certain areas? Pleasure is a total body experience. To truly satisfy your needs you must view the whole body as an instrument of pleasure. When we see our sexuality as a part of our entire being — body, mind, heart and spirit — we discover a thousand new ways to be fulfilled.

Talk is the ear's food.
Jamaican proverb

August 4

When we say "I respect you", what we are saying is "I see you as a person, both the flaws and other aspects which make you unique as an individual." True respect means that your concerns and feelings are mine too. My judgment is not required, just my feelings. I respect you enough to appreciate the person you are becoming. But for me to respect you, I myself must be centred, I myself must have confidence in who I am and my potential. To respect you, I must respect myself.

1991: Joe Harker, formerly deputy editor of The Voice newspaper, launches his own rival black paper, *Black Briton*, at the age of 29.

The price of your hat ain't the measure of your brain.
African-American saying

August 5

Responsibility is another aspect of love. Not the kind which is imposed upon us by external forces such as the state, institutions or family, which can lead to negative and confrontational feelings. Instead true responsibility is a voluntary giving of the self, a selfless act. To be responsible is to be ready, willing and able to respond. The loving person feels that the problems of another are also their problems. The pain, suffering, joy and elation of another you share.

1910: Legendary African-American actor Bert Williams stars in the independent black film, *Darktown Jubilee.*

I feel myself in need of the inspiring strains of ancient lore. My heart to lift, my empty mind to feed, and all the world explore.
George Moses Horton

August 6

1962: Jamaica's black, gold and green national flag raised for the first time.

Communication is to a relationship what breathing is to life. At its best it allows us to deal with problems before they become serious, ensures our mental and emotional health and, increases intimacy between friends and lovers. It promotes understanding and prevents ill-feeling. Every relationship in our lives can benefit from it. At work, our concerns and ideas can be aired. Within the family, arguments and disharmony need not arise. We may have been born with a mouth and learnt how to talk, but good communication is the product of effort and practice.

I am alive and a sensual being. I am entitled to pleasure.

August 7

1904: Dr Ralph J. Bunche wins the Nobel peace prize.

The expression of feelings has been made difficult for some of us because we have grown up in an environment where people have not openly expressed their feelings and, for men, it has been deemed "unmasculine". It takes strength of character for us to overcome such obstacles. Feelings define your essence. When you can properly express your loneliness, fear, joy and anticipation, that is when you are ready for a deep and real relationship.

While we are awake we should allow our hearts to bear the shame of being seen living.
Efua T. Sutherland

August 8

One of the nicest gifts we can give to ourselves, friends and family, is the gift of listening. We are all familiar with the feeling of frustration when we are not being listened to or understood. Communication is about sending and receiving messages. If the message is not received, communication has broken down. This doesn't just mean standing still long enough to hear the words, nor keeping your mouth shut and your ears open. You must listen "without prejudice", allow those dear to you to speak their mind. You may find this hard to begin with, but you will be surprised at how much you understand of what is said.

1980: Ronald Hope becomes the first black police Inspector in the UK.

I am not pretending to be me. I am only what I am.

August 9

In the realm of human relationships there are few certainties, but one of them is the presence of conflict. As there are no people born with exactly the same desires, this possibility is inevitable. But unfortunately most of us have been brought up in homes where conflict has been expressed in either uncontrollable rage or physical violence. As yet we have not learnt the value of conflict between people. Conflict exposes unrealistic expectations, shakes the status quo, and leads to change, growth and better understanding. When we learn to handle conflict positively we learn that the outcome will leave two victors.

1988: Bill Cosby donates $20 million to Spelman College in the U.S.

I am my mother's daughter and the drums of Africa still beat in my heart.
Mary McLeod Bethune

August 10

1945: Irene Ighodaro qualifies as a doctor. The first female doctor in Sierra Leone.

Just as no two people's fingerprints are the same, no two people's needs for intimacy are similar. Every relationship we enter into, is going to be a totally different experience from any other. For the relationship to blossom we must understand space, a clear demarcation. Although we are an "item", clear personal boundaries must exist so that each person is allowed the freedom to be themselves. For a healthy and prosperous relationship, it takes two independent, self-reliant people who can gain fulfilment both within and externally. We must appreciate each other's need to "be" as much as we value and cherish our own.

Lies are told and legends made. Phoenix rises unafraid.
G. Brooks

August 11

1899: African-American J.A. Burr obtains the patent for the lawn mower.

When you have watched people throwing tantrums, whining and complaining about a situation, yet not taking any action to bring about change, don't you just want to tell them to GROW UP! Make a positive distinction between childlike emotions — playfulness, joy and exuberance, and childish behaviour — spoilt, infantile. This kind of behaviour befits no one and is destructive. It's time to get in control, become mature, GROW UP!

This is just life; it's not to be cried over, just understood.
Ralph Ellison

August 12

We have the tendency to be "fair weather friends". When people are nice, pleasant and undemanding, we welcome them with open arms. But as soon as the tide turns and they are a "problem" we seem more reluctant to help. Instead of walking away and feeling indifferent to their pain, we should turn towards them to learn the true meaning of unconditional love. We learn to give more when the other is helpless, weak and in need of our support. Give of yourself to your friends when it is really needed.

1948: West Indies cricketer George Headley becomes the first man to score two centuries in one test match.

You are the ancient builders of civilisation. Before there was civilisation, you were there, and when civilisation was built, your fathers built it.
Louis Farrakhan

August 13

We run ourselves ragged trying to take charge of situations and other people. Stop and let yourself breathe. Your first priority is to yourself. Take charge of your body. Take charge over your emotions and feel content, enthusiastic and fulfilled.

1979: Lloyd King founds Hackney Education Development Society (HEADS), and spearheads the campaign for better library facilities in Hackney.

Cleanse your soul of hate as I have done mine.

August 14

1883: Ernest E. Just is born. He is destined to become a marine biologist, and to investigate the genetic make-up of animals, and cellular theory.

One may not reach the dawn save by the path of the night.
Kahlil Gibran

When next you encounter someone and say to yourself, "I hate you", try and understand what it is about yourself that you see in this person and don't like to be confronted with. When you say "I love you", think what it is that you love about yourself that you see in this person. When you ask the questions, you begin to learn even more about yourself, and your relationship with YOU and others will be more enjoyable and fulfiling.

August 15

1907: Nat Love, alias Deadwood Dick, publishes his memoirs, a popular book which tells of his exciting and unusual life as a black cowboy in the Wild West.

Return to yourself. Keep your powers alive.

Why hold onto grievances? Why hold onto such toxic waste? For give it away. Heal the wounds. Release it. It's not worth holding onto. When you think of forgiving, think of it literally as FOR GIVING. For — in favour, of giving — to give. When we forgive other people, who are we giving to? To the other person, yes, but to ourselves also. So when you forgive another you are in favour of giving to yourself. Forgiving is the way forward. Forgive your enemy, so that you can move on. YOU'VE GOT WORK TO DO!

August 16

Your word is one of the most precious things you can own. Think twice before giving it away. Once you have given it do everything in your power to uphold it. Like a broken cup, a broken word cannot hold much substance. Your word is like a grain of sand, take care that the wind doesn't blow it back in your face. Only make agreements you intend to keep. Fulfill every one you make. When you keep your word, keep it safe, true and strong and its effect will be magnificently powerful.

1956: The first UK black athlete to gain international recognition at the Olympics is Micheal Bailey, winning a bronze medal.

The trials of life are meaningless unless you learn from them.

August 17

A clenched fist is similar to a clenched heart. We make it extremely difficult to receive anything good, positive and loving. When we open the fist, we have a hand. At times we may think that a waving fist, full of the bitterness of resentment, is the way we will receive. But a waving fist often meets with another waving fist.

1887: Marcus Garvey, great black leader, motivator and Pan-African advocate, born in Jamaica.

A man is not as much as he feels he is, but as much as he feels.
Jean Toomer

August 18

1894: African-American W.U. Moody takes out the patent for the oil heater/cooker.

I believe in the brotherhood of all men, but I don't believe in wasting brotherhood on anyone who doesn't want to practice it with me.
Brotherhood is a two-way street.
Malcolm X

It kills the spirit to be constantly depressed. When you're at your lowest ebb remember, the only way is up. Upliftment is at hand, all around you. Let simple pleasures fill your life. Go for a stroll and take a closer look at LIFE. Take a closer look at that large building that you pass every day, but which you have never really seen. Notice the beauty of its architecture. Take a closer look at that tree you've hardly noticed all this time. What kind of a tree is it? Look up in its branches and see how many types of wildlife feed off it. Look up in the night sky and smile. Find your particular star and see how bright it's burning for you. UPLIFTMENT IS ALL AROUND YOU. Life is what you allow to happen, but life is also what slips by every day.

August 19

1967: Margaret Busby prints poems with a friend and sells them on the streets of London. In 1968 she sets up Allison & Busby, publishing *The Spook Who Sat By The Door,* **and continues to publish world authors.**

Be generous, and you will be prosperous.
Proverbs 11, v.25

Albert liked music, Dizzy Gillespie through to Jimi Hendrix. He played music when the sun shone and when the rain beat a rhythm on the window pane. When his children were born, he played them music all through their lives. When they grew up and left home his wife asked him, "Are you disappointed that none of our children became musicians?" He smiled and replied, "No. If we don't share our passions with our children, how can they learn to have passions of their own?"

August 20

The kente cloth has many significancies. For me, far from Africa, it reminds me that Britain might be my country, but not my land. When I wear the kente cloth, I wear it with pride and it gives me the deep sense of belonging to a tradition that stretches back thousands of years. And it represents a feeling of possessing just a little bit of Africa, that Africa is mine! In my life, the kente cloth reflects a magnificent coming together of many things.

1966: Jesse Jackson spearheads Operation Breadbasket in Chicago, to encourage minority jobs. In 1971 he starts Operation PUSH (People United to Serve Humanity).

Love is two people feeding each other, not one living on the soul of the other, like a parasite.

August 21

In African cultures the birth of a child is an event worthy of celebration, shared not only between the parents and other siblings, but aunts, uncles, nieces and nephews. The care and upbringing of that child is a matter of concern and responsibility for everyone. We must re-establish the "extended family". A family of mother, father, grandparents, aunts, nieces, brothers, sisters and cousins who give each other support just because we are family.

1967: The East African Economic Community is established, with Kenya, Tanzania and Uganda sharing railways, airlines, harbours currency and telecommunications.

One daddy fe 20 pickney, but twenty pickney no fe one daddy.
Caribbean proverb

August 22

1948: Sebastian Clarke born. He went on to write the first UK documentary on reggae shown on BBC TV, then wrote London Weekend TV show on Jamaican music.

There are fifty kinds of lunacy, but only one kind of common sense.
Bantu proverb

The thing that inspires me the most, is the love I bear people of colour. Hemmed, circumscribed with every imaginable obstacle in our way, blocked and held down by fear and prejudices, we still emerge strong and noble. When I hear of successes, however small or great, by people of colour, I feel proud and want to achieve even greater things than I had thought possible.

August 23

1974: Gaspar K. Martindale is a founder member of the Black People's Information Centre based in Ladbroke Grove, London, giving local people access to computers and other equipment.

There's nothing wrong with loving yourself.

Sisterly love is the most basic and fundamental love. Sisterly love is solidarity. Sisterly love is responsibility, care, respect, knowledge, and the concern for each other's development. Sisterly love transcends superficial differences. Class, race and EVEN gender are irrelevant to sisterly love. We all need help from time to time, today you, tomorrow me. You could start an informal network of sistas who help each other in your neighbourhood. But even if you are never in the position to help me, I still have sisterly love for you.

August 24

If our relationships are to grow strong we must consciously put aside time in order to be with them. Not just in body but in spirit as well. If we are truly committed to the growth and development of our partnerships, then we must recognise the importance of time. Time not cluttered up with affairs of work or social obligations. Time spent talking, hugging, sharing our dreams and our aspirations, time spent in connection. Time spent finding mutual ground.

1974: Ermin Le-kin, social worker, spearheads the campaign "Soul Kids" to promote black fostering and adopting in the UK.

Sometimes I feel like a motherless child, a long way from home.

August 25

Due to our expectations, or lack of them, in relationships we are often willing to put up with bad behaviour. We do everything in our power to please. We forgive lies, unthoughtfulness and even abuse. We give and give until there is nothing left and realise too late that we are worthy of more. We achieve nothing, yet a little bit of us dies in the process. In trying to make our partner happy, we must ensure that we save a little love for ourselves.

1899: J.H. Dickinson takes out the patent for the pianola, an early version of the modern day piano.

Old as she was, she still missed her daddy sometimes.
Gloria Naylor

August 26

1831: Sam Sharp leads a slave rebellion against the British in Jamaica.

Slave driver, the tables have turned, Catch a fire and you will get burned.
Bob Marley

Marcia liked Kwame, but her friends told her he was overweight. She also liked Stedman, but they thought she could find someone who was less of a slob. When she was with D, they told her he was going nowhere fast. When she was with Jamal, everyone told her he was a gold-digger. When she met Lloyd someone told her he had a child and was looking for a mother/wife. And when she met Terry, who she had a great deal of fun with and who was happy doing the cooking and the cleaning, her friends advised her that he was too feminine (that he was a "maama man" to be precise) and was looking for a "sista" not a lover. Now Marcia is alone and doesn't understand why she listened to her friends in the first place.

August 27

1942: Poet Louise Bennett rejects formal English by publishing her collection in Jamaican dialect.

When we seh smaddy 'boogoo-yagga', everybody know seh dat him outta order An' if we seh dem 'boonoonoonoos' yuh know seh dat dem nice.
Louise Bennett

When you examine your life, do you find that you are the director or just an actor? Are you actively involved in structuring your life or are you going along with someone else's plan? Is your life made up of someone else's desires, demands and needs? Are you the star in your life, or are you the understudy? Do you go with the moment, or do you refer to another? Is life a daily challenge which you relish or is it just a chore? Are you tailoring the script or are you scripted by the tale? Are you mouthing someone else's words, thinking somebody else's thoughts? Why don't you sit in the director's chair for a change and take charge of your life? Now that's the movie we're all dying to see.

August 28

What kind of song are you singing today? Are you singing a song of woe? A litany inspired by men or women who have done you wrong? Are you singing a song of wrongs and injustices done to you, your parents or even grandparents? Are you singing to an audience? Is your song filled with fear of the past or hope for the future? Is yours a happy song, filled with meaning and tenderness, or a cacophony of sound? Listen keenly to your song. Is it a song full of disappointment, a eulogy of bitter-sweet love? Then learn the lesson, rewrite the verses with positive words, and move on.

1963: Martin Luther King Jr. makes his world famous "I have a dream" speech at the Lincoln Memorial in front of tens of thousands.

All lies die when the truth is told.

August 29

Before you set off on your great quest for Mr or Miss Right, stand in front of the mirror and take a good, hard look at the person that is on offer. If you met yourself on the street would you immediately think "Mmm, I would like to get to know you"? Would you want this person in your life for a day, a week, a month, a year, for ever? Ask yourself, "When I get angry today are they echoes of before? Do I feel confident enough to ask for what I don't have, and am I prepared to have my needs met by another? Am I rooted in my centre, do I trust myself?" If most of your responses are No, then you still have some work to do. As you would want to be with the best, love yourself enough to be your best.

1987: Rita Dove wins the Pulitzer Prize for her poetry.

And she had nothing to fall back on; not maleness not ladyhood, not anything. And out of profound desolation of her reality she may well have invented herself.
Toni Morrison

August 30

You do not understand who I am if you think I have forgotten who I am... I am a black woman, the daughter of hard-working parents who had to struggle to make ends meet. I am a black woman who always had to fight for everything she got. I had to fight for an education. I had to fight for a home. I had to fight for my children and I had to fight for a job. I didn't start out in the position I have achieved today. If you think I have forgotten that, you are wrong.

Da blacker da berry
Da sweeter da juice.

August 31

When Maxine and Lawrence separated, Lawrence vowed that he would not stop being a father. He called his daughter at least once a week. He would send her post cards or notes, to give her encouragement about her studies and to emphasise that he still loved her. Lawrence treated his visiting times like gold. If he was due at four o'clock, he came fifteen minutes earlier. At our hands, our children learn trust. If we let them down, how can they learn to believe in anything we tell them? How can they learn to respect us or respect themselves? When we ask our children to trust us they open their hearts to us. If we crush that hope when will they ever learn to trust another with their hearts?

It's punishment to be compelled to do what one doesn't wish.
Alice D. Nelson

September 1

Child rearing isn't glamorous, there are no perks or fringe benefits, paid holidays, no company car or pension fund. Not even a chance of promotion. There is no social status. So where is the incentive to be a parent? Payment comes when our children come first to us with their newest thought. We receive increments when we help in their development. We reap our rewards when we nurture their spirit and minds. We gain job satisfaction when we enable them to be people in their own right. And we get paid in full every time our children tell us that they love us.

1853: Elizabeth T. Greenfield sings a second concert for African-Americans after they are barred from her original concert.

I only want to reclaim myself.
Nikki Giovanni

September 2

Love is not just about flowers and candlelight, but about finding that "safe place" within to which we can withdraw for shelter. When you have found that safe place, furnish it with love and remember how to find your way back to it so that you can always shelter there with or without a partner.

1987: Diane Abbott becomes the first African-Caribbean female member of the British parliament.

We must redefine ourselves, state new values and goals, so that we may purify our souls of four hundred years of mis-education.

September 3

1990: Neville Clare receives an award for his services to the community in founding OSCAR, the Organisation for Sickle Cell Anaemia Research.

God made the sea, we make the ship; He made the wind, we make the sail; He made the calm, we make oars.
Swahili proverb

By a mixture of respect, admiration and fear we place our parents on a pedestal. We may never have got to know them as ordinary everyday people, capable of feeling fear or joy, but the relationship we have with our parents sets the direction for all others we will have in life. As we try to sort through the mixed emotions of our upbringing we have to keep in mind that our parents had no handbook. They didn't do too badly considering. Take the chance to talk to them of their lives. Not just about idle reminiscences, but their experiences and encounters. Get closer to your parents now. It is important because they are not just our parents, they are our elders. Their past can serve as our signpost to the future.

September 4

1848: African-American Lewis Latimer born. Destined to invent the carbon filament and the electric light bulb.

Lovers are like two turtle doves, always feeding each other.
Swahili proverb

The two main decisions we make about relationships are a) to begin them, and b) to end them. When we begin a relationship, we expect it to nurture us, help us to evolve and give us pleasure. We hope we will never have to end it. But then we discover that relationships can be unbalanced, harmful, negative and depleting of our resources and self-esteem. It is time to make that other big decision! When we end a relationship it is not a sign of defeat or failure, simply admit that, "I have learned more about myself by being with you, but the lesson is over now and for my happiness I must move on." And the next time you choose to start a relationship, begin by saying, "I am complete in myself and would like to share myself with you, receiving your gifts and learning and enhancing your life."

September 5

There are a lot of manipulative people out there whose intent is to skillfully play you like pieces in a game of chess. There are also masters of illusion who delude, confuse and destroy lives. The minute you reclaim you for yourself, no one can have any kind of power over you. Stake a claim of your own on yourself, for happiness and love.

1995: Responding to the call of Minister Louis Farrakhan, a million black men march on Washington DC to affirm their belief in the black family.

A friend is the one who praises you when you are not there.
Yoruba proverb

September 6

I will smile again.
I will see the dawn again.
I will rise again.
I will be filled with joy again.
I have the power to define and create my inner state of happiness again.
There is no room for FEAR in my life.

1956: Trinidadian born Pearl Connor-Mogotsi, establishes the first black theatre agency in London.

A good conversation is better than a good bed.
Galla proverb

September 7

1963: SANROC established in South Africa, dedicated to destroying racial discrimination within sports.

The highest good is like that of water. The goodness of water is that it benefits the ten thousand creatures; yet itself does not scramble. **The Way and it's Power**

Out of many — one people. When we recognise our similarities instead of focusing on our differences, as a people we can begin to see the improvements we strive for.

September 8

1984: Lydia Simmons becomes the first black female mayor in Britain.

Your children are not your children. They are the sons and daughters of Life's longing for itself. **The Prophet Kahlil Gibran**

When it is love that motivates us, we discover that every small gift, gesture and thought that endears us to our partner is inspirational. Each gentle touch, every loving word, is the fuel that we need to take us there - wherever we want to go.

September 9

Out of sight — never out of mind. True friendship in its purest form is an unconditional love. A deep compulsion to aid, share and cherish and understand that special person you highly regard as your friend. A good friend is like an oasis in the desert.

1948: 491 men and one woman arrived in England from Jamaica on the S.S. Empire Windrush. These pioneers opened the way for black migration from the British colonies.

It's wise to know when one does not know.

September 10

Say what you mean, mean what you say. So often we are misunderstood causing much distress and confusion. The word can be a mighty sword when used with wisdom.

1846: 30 black families successfully farmed the 40 acres in upstate New York, granted to them by the American Government.

It's time to shine your brilliant light on the lives of our mothers, who for too long have been left in the shadows of history.

September 11

1984: Bernard Wiltshire pioneers the first supplementary school in the London borough of Hackney.

Let me show you the world like you've never seen it before, shining, genuine, splendid. Climb on board this magic carpet ride and open your eyes wide to a whole new world. On your return, you'll never be the same again. Once you've seen that magic world where true love goes, you'll never again settle for love that's less than true.

You can't be nobody but who you are.
August Wilson

September 12

1983: Dr Alexa Canady becomes the first African-American female Neurosurgeon.

Children are not our property. They may live in our house, eat off our plates and play a major part in our everyday lives, but they do not belong to us. They are all the Creator's children but have been put in our care. The Creator expects us to teach them well, shower them with love and understanding, and instill in them a thirst for knowledge and justice — then let them go.

Gifts seem small compared with giving of yourself. That's truly giving.

September 13

We all face many battles in life: injustice, inequality, prejudice, dissatisfaction and personal turmoil are a few. The hardest, and possibly the most important battle, is the one we face with our children, to reassure them of their worth and value, to allay their fears about the outside world, to reinforce the spirit within them, to promote individual thought and reflection. If we win this battle, our jobs as parents will have been successful.

1884: African-American W. Johnson receives the patent for the egg beater.

The gifts of the earth are abundant. Be satisfied.

September 14

Eshe came home crying. Boys at school had teased her about the style of her hair, and the markings on her face. They said her hair looked like snakes, and that the markings on her face made her look ugly. Her mother told her that there were some people who would not appreciate the beauty of her hair, or understand the cultural significance of the tribal marks. She told her of the bond that they created between Eshe and their people. She lovingly stroked her hair and cheeks. Her child looked at her and said, "They make me different and special." Her mother smiled and said, "Yes." If we as adults do not have a strong sense of ourselves, how can we hope to instill in our children a pride in who they are, what they can achieve, and who they can become?

1981: Jewel Jackson McCabe forms the National Coalition of 100 Black Women to increase voter registration in the U.S. Today, no serious politician can ignore them.

Anyt'ing me seh, ounu seh 'proud to be black...'
Crucial Robbie

September 15

I need time to think. When we retreat into our minds and hibernate, we do so to re-emerge with a clearer idea of the big picture and our role in it. Silence and solitude are essential but isolating. You need to let those close to you know that you haven't gone for good. So when next you need to be alone with your thoughts, leave a notice saying: "Gone thinking, back in a while!"

Such as I am, I am a precious gift.
Zora Neale Hurston

September 16

When we leave a relationship or lose someone we love, we feel bereft, desolate and isolated. But how can we say that we have lost them when they have given us the most precious thing one human being can give to another, a whisper of their spirit? IT'S ALL GOOD.

Remember that praise is more fun than criticism.

September 17

Sex is an expression of our essential selves, individual, multiple, beautiful. When shared earnestly and deeply, it is one of life's greatest gifts.

September 18

An eighteen-year-old girl was talking to her lecturer. He asked her about the choices she had made for her career. Her response was, "I would like to be a psychologist." She went on to explain that in order for her to qualify a long period of study was to be undertaken. She also felt that she might be too old by that time. The lecturer pondered on the response for a while, then asked her,

"How long would it take you to become a psychologist?"

Her reply was, "Seven years."

He next asked her, "What age would you be?"

"Twenty-five," she said.

Finally he asked her, "How old will you be in seven years if you don't become a psychologist?" Naturally the only response she could give was "Twenty-five!" Time waits for no one.

September 19

Sometimes, not wanting to offend, we say "yes" or "maybe" to the impossible, causing disappointment and confusion. Don't be afraid to say "NO!"

September 20

When we learn to respect others as we respect ourselves we learn that people are too valuable to possess. We all have to be allowed to make our own choices and take our own chances. We each need the opportunity to make our own mistakes and be who we want to be.

September 21

Some of us are hampered by the way we have been raised up; criticism, sarcasm, loneliness and rejection. We must learn to be a hundred times more willing to express gratitude and love than to express contempt. If we don't we are destined to raise generations who will never know the feeling of being cherished.

1916: The U.S. National Association of Colored Women save the home of black hero Frederick Douglass from reposession for the benefit of future generations.

As a South African I am endowed by nature with a strength much greater than my size.
Miriam Makeba

September 22

Anyone who has ever been in love can relate to the rollercoaster of passion and pain that I am now going through. Barely have I celebrated passion than pain comes knocking at my door. Let us meet at the crossroads where we can shed pain and make sure it does not follow us on our journeys. Women of colour need to unload the baggage taken into relationships, otherwise the cycle of distrust, abuse, pain and anger will be perpetuated.Who knows you better than yourself? Who loves you better than you, and who do you live with twenty-four hours a day, seven days a week?

KEEP YOUR OWN COUNSEL.
LISTEN TO YOUR INNER VOICE.
TRUST YOUR OWN INSTINCT.

1805: Through land deals, Edwin P. McCabe establishes 25 black communities in Oklahoma.

Now, women forget all those things they don't want to remember, and remember everything they don't want to forget. The dream is the truth. Then they act and do things accordingly.
Zora Neale Hurston

September 23

1886: Lucy Laney establishes a school in Augusta, Georgia, at a time when the state neglects the education of its black children, and runs it for 50 years. Mary McLeod Bethune (soon to become the world's richest woman), is a graduate.

Laughter gives confidence; its absence causes dispute.

They owe us more than they could ever pay back. They stole our language, they stole our culture. They stole our mothers and fathers and took our names away from us. They stole all those things yet we still survived, because try as hard as they might, they couldn't steal the SOULS of black folk. When you are at your wits end, search your temple within and you too will find the key to survival.

September 24

1990: After years of trying to get her foot in the door as a secretary at London's Capital Radio, Angie Greaves realizes her ambition by hosting her own inspirational morning show on Choice FM.

To conquer others needs strength. To conquer yourself is even harder.

The most powerful yet gentle thing you possess is a smile? It is a universal language. Make the smile you give today a bright one, it may make all the difference.

September 25

When we are a true friend we must be willing to have our advice ignored, and still be willing to give it again.

1959: West Indian Standing Conference established after the Notting Hill riots, to promote harmony within the community.

It is necessary to achieve freedom by any means necessary.
Malcolm X

September 26

Humour has a way of breaking down barriers and revealing the universal truths of all our lives. When we take a light-hearted look at ourselves, we realise that situations that we thought were crises were really just hiccups in life's multi-textured pattern.

1957: Nine black children determined to claim their right to education, help end school segregation by making their way to Central High School, Little Rock, Arkansas, despite the white mob threatening them.

The tree cannot stand without its roots.

September 27

1896: African-American George Washington Carver receives his science degree at 33, then goes on to revolutionise the agricultural industry, breaking down the components of the peanut.

Only the fool will laugh at you when you try to enlighten him for his own good.

One of the most destructive emotions is jealousy. When we acknowledge the feelings of jealousy we have, we begin to vanquish the demons we have in us. Demons of self doubt, lack of fulfilment, lack of purpose. By facing our demons we attend to our needs and gain knowledge of ourselves.

September 28

1891: African-American J. Standard receives the patent for the refrigerator.

You may believe in your convictions and be convicted for your beliefs. Having courage of your conviction may cause alienation and loss of possessions. Hold on fast to your beliefs — recognise your value. Keep the inner light burning bright.

If you itch scratch; if you still itch, take a bath.
Bill Cosby

September 29

No woman is an island. Many hands make light work.

1988: Sharon Atkin becomes first black woman on the Association of London Authorities Policy Committee.

A sure way for someone to lift himself up is by helping to lift someone else.
Booker T. Washington

September 30

We try to be independent, strong and tough. We have been taught to cope. We struggle to make strides forward. We try so hard that we lose sight of the fact that we are not alone, that we have each other. We need each other for assurance and support, to laugh with or just dream with. Together we are strengthened.

1960: Alhaji Tafewa Balewa becomes the first president of Nigeria, after independence from British colonial rule.

Talk about it only enough to do it. Dream about it only enough to feel it. Think about it only enough to understand it. Contemplate it only enough to be it.

October 1

1798: James Forten single-handedly establishes a sail-making business, and invents a sail-handling device.

When your children grow up in an environment where commitment and dedication is not just talked about but lived to the fullness, it can't help but take root in their beings. The best lessons and the best sermons are those that are lived.

Life is what your thoughts make of it.

October 2

1821: African-American Thomas L. Jennings gains patent for dry cleaning clothes.

I'm folding up my little dreams within my heart tonight And praying I may soon forget the torture of their sight.
Georgia Douglass Johnson

Be a parent filled with playfulness, understanding, direction and tolerance. When you come home in the evening, kiss your children. Sit down at the table with them to eat dinner. Joke with them and laugh with them. Take them out to interesting places every now and then and teach them all you know about life, people and, in particular, about living. Teach them all the things you feel are necessary in leading a good life and a life that would contribute to society.

October 3

We all have dreams that we want to come true, but how many of us follow those dreams with the single-minded determination that is needed to make them come true? Often we start off with great passion and zeal. Somehow along the way we lose interest. The stars are there to be reached if we want to reach them.

1834: David Ruggles opens the first black bookshop in New York.

If you only care enough for a result you will almost certainly obtain it. If you wish to be rich, you will be rich.
William James

October 4

My parents had me so convinced that I was precious that by the time I found out that I was nothing, it was already too late — I knew I was something.

1834: African-American Henry Blair receives patent for corn-planting machine.

Wealth is the product of your capacity to think.

October 5

Perception is the only real difference between those people of colour who get what they desire and those who do not.

October 6

You and I are like nothing under the sun. No jewel is as rare as you, no amount of gold can measure. You are unique, one of a kind. The wealth of beauty that is in you is deeper than the deepest point in the sea; your love is more vast than the horizon. Your capability is limitless. Value yourself. Extol your virtues every day of your life. Sweep through life like a majestic galleon. Let kindness be your assets, let joy be your collateral and, love the currency with which you purchase life.

October 7

We must accept ourselves for the person we are now, not who we are waiting to become. Otherwise we are divided between two souls, two thoughts, unreconciled yearnings and ambitions. Two conflicting ideals in the same dark body is sure to play havoc with your life.

1920s-30s: Until her death in 1934, Maggie Walker was on the board of Consolidated Bank, an amalgamation of several black banks.

If you're not getting better, you're getting worse.

October 8

If your life makes you unhappy then do whatever is necessary to change it, be at peace with yourself. The present is well within your grasp. Embrace all that allows you to grow in experience and love.

1933: H. Naylor Fitzhugh earns his business degree from Harvard. His expertise is used to set up *Black Enterprise* magazine in 1974.

Only your friend knows your secrets, so only he can reveal it.

October 9

1995: Ken Saro-Wiwa dies fighting for the rights of the 300,000 Ogoni people of Nigeria, against the multi-national oil companies exploiting their land.

Praise, love and approval are the great motivators in life, helping to affirm our sense of self worth. The spirit blossoms with renewed confidence where love abounds. A person who can give praise when it is deserved shows that they value themselves and others around them. And when we meet with approval we realise the HOPE that people see in us.

If it's hard, then do it hard.
Les Brown

October 10

1893: African-Americans establish the Alabama Penny Savings and Loan Co. in Birmingham. It survives the economic depression of that year.

If the goal which you wish to reach requires you to give your all — then give it. Give it unstintingly and unswervingly, because the outcome will be well worth the effort you made. With dedication and the spirit of enthusiasm, obstacles become stepping stones.

Nothing great was ever achieved without enthusiasm.

October 11

The way in which you spend your life energy should not destroy your soul.

1970: Joseph L. Searles becomes the first black man at the New York Stock Exchange.

I was not born with a silver spoon in my mouth, but with a clothes basket upon my head.
Maggie Lena Walker

October 12

We are the ones who create boundaries for ourselves. By not allowing ourselves to dream of the infinite possibilities. Each one of us must realise our power. Through faith we can accomplish whatever our hearts desire.

1971: Johnson cosmetics company is the first black owned and run company to be floated on the New York Stock Exchange.

Up you mighty race, you can accomplish much.
Marcus Garvey

October 13

1980: Robert Johnson's, Black Entertainment Television (BET) is America's first black TV station, run and hosted by African-Americans.

Nothing in the world is so pleasing to see as black pride. No one loves to see it more than me.

Be ever-ready. Opportunity may only knock once!!!

October 14

1993: At his death, African-American Reginald Lewis's personal fortune is estimated at $400 million. He is listed in *Forbes Magazine* as one of America's 400 wealthiest people.

One chance is all you need.
Jesse Owens

Rejoice in the force of life, of life itself, conscious of every breath you take, feeling the lightest breeze against your cheek.

October 15

Life is an opportunity, grab it.
Life is beauty, admire it.
Life is a challenge, confront it.
Life is a duty, fulfil it.
Life is a game, take part in it.
Life is costly, value it.
Life is wealth, look after it.
Life is love, express it.
Life is mystery, discover it.
Life is a promise, uphold it.
Life is sorrow, get over it.
Life is a song, sing it.
Life is a struggle, accept it.
Life is a tragedy, overcome it.
Life is an adventure, pursue it.
Life is precious, do not destroy it.
Life is life, fight for it.

1957: Southern Christian Leadership Conference founded with Ella Baker, the grandchild of a former slave who refused to marry the light-skinned man of her master's choice, at its helm.

Live! and have your blooming in the noise of the whirlwind.

October 16

In order to succeed in life you must first know where you wish to go.

1932: *The Conjure Man Dies* by Rudolph Fisher is the first African-American murder mystery.

The believer begins with herself.
Berber proverb

October 17

What becomes of the broken hearted, depends on how soon we heal our wounds. Healing cleanses the body and the spirit, without it heartache will cling to you like a monkey on your back. A broken heart will force you to retreat into a world of loneliness, but healing will help to draw you out again. Healing dwells in every corner of the world. It dwells amongst that unofficial sisterhood called Strong Black Women whose reputation in the face of adversity is known worldwide. And it resides in you, in your inner power, where it lies side by side with your knowledge and continuing faith in Strong Black Women. Let the healing continue! You'll seem stronger and taller, really ready to take on the challenges.

October 18

Say it...
"I have the power to shape my own destiny. Nothing prevents me from receiving the bountiful gifts the Creator has in store for me, but myself. I now remove all feelings of unworthiness and proclaim my desires with a firm and unshaking voice which speaks the truth of my heart. Success is there for me if I only try and attain it. In the act of trying, I acknowledge that I deserve my desires, and in achieving them I am thankful and praise those who have helped me on my way. It is the will of the Creator that I reach my goals without malice towards others, and that I share in others' triumphs with jubilant heart, as I would wish them to do with me."

October 19

Whatever goodness I expect from others, I will first search for that goodness myself. If I cannot nurture those feelings of love and fulfilment within myself, I cannot successfully nurture others.

1983:
Journalist Marc
Wadsworth is
a founder
member of
Black
Sections in
the UK
Labour Party.

*It is not only
giants who do
great things.*

October 20

I am rich when I have inner peace, and am
    balanced.
I have wealth when I recognise my weakness in
    order to make myself strong.
I amass a fortune when I share my joy.
I multiply my wealth when I realise my potential.
I consolidate my assets when I spend time with
      myself.
I increase in value when I invest in myself.

No bank can hold my fortune.
I need no security guards to protect me.

1964: Dr
Kenneth
Kaunda leads
Zambia to
independence
from British
colonial rule.

*Leave the battle
to God and rest
your head upon
your hand.*
Yoruba proverb

October 21

1938: Sixty-seven middle class black women march on the White House demanding a say in the running of the country.

Save some of what you've got - result happiness. Spend what you ain't got - result misery!

Take a moment in the day when you can shut your eyes and quietly say to yourself, YES. I say, YES to my personal success. Yes to my good health. Yes to my clean living. Yes to the spirit that evolves with every experience. Yes to my prosperity. I fling my arms wide in anticipation of the wonders that will be mine in time.

October 22

1877: African-American Garrett A. Morgan, inventor of the traffic light, is born.

If one is continually surviving the worst that life can bring, one eventually ceases to be controlled by a fear of what life can bring.
James Baldwin

By keeping a firm check on our finances we can prevent a great deal of worry and stress. Money, and the lack of it, can dominate our entire lives, eating slowly away at our spirit. By taking control of our purse strings we effectively take control of our lives. Add up your bank balance regularly, however tedious it may be, fill in the tax return forms before the deadline. Account for every penny you have spent today. To be responsible is not easy, but it is even harder to be a slave to money. Money allows us to do so much. If we do not take control of it, it will inevitably take control of us.

October 23

In order to cultivate love, harmony, health and tranquillity let your life be a prayer. Your every thought, movement and deed. Your sorrow, your sadness, every breath you take and every day you live, let it be a prayer. Let the work of your hands be a prayer. The temple that is your body will radiate the light of the Creator. When everything you think, do or say becomes one continuous prayer, a golden stream of blessings flows towards you. Only then will all that you do or say be protected from darkness and injury. Because there is light in prayer.

1942: Margaret Walker's, *For My People* wins the Yale Young Poets Award, the first African-American to do so.

I have my yearnings, You have your longings, Let's get together in harmony.

October 24

The way in which we approach problems determines whether we solve the problem or not. Believe in your ability to solve every problem, and who knows what great revelations you will discover.

1937: Joe Louis, the son of an Alabama sharecropper, becomes the first African-American heavyweight boxing champ since Jack Johnson in 1905.

Success, is getting what you want and happiness is wanting what you get.

October 25

1974: Alex Pascall, OBE, presents the first black radio programme in Britain, *Black Londoners*. In 1985, he starts the foundation for European Carnival Cities.

Show your class in everything you do. In your coming in and going out - show your class.

As all the stamps in your passport testify, you have travelled far and wide. You have tripped the light fantastic in Paris and haggled for a carpet in the old bazaars of Istanbul. However, the only passport that allows you unlimited travel is life and, the trips of real significance are the ones you make daily, the experiences you gain and people you meet. Allow your spirit to roam and you will be amazed where it takes you — to the far flung corners of the known universe and to the still quiet place where no plane or ship can go.

October 26

1891: African-American P.B. Downing receives the patent for a street letter box.

Time and time again, I am filled up with all that I thought life might be - glorious moment upon glorious moment of contentment and joy and love running into each other...
Jamaica Kincaid

The search for happiness is universal, considered to be so important by the founding fathers of America that they wrote it into the Declaration of Independence. But like mythological beasts of old, there are many sightings of happiness but none of the witnesses can agree on the description. We run hither and thither in search of it. Everyone wants to be happy, but few ever feel that they have found happiness, so we continue our search. Each of us must FIND our own happiness, or MAKE our own happiness. True happiness has nothing to do with what you see in the outside world, it comes from within.

October 27

When we open our hearts to the fullest they are filled to the greatest capacity, when we only open them slightly they will only be slightly filled. When you open your mind fully it will fill to the brim with wonderful things, but close it and nothing goes in. Open your life wide and fill it with people and experiences that enhance it. Expand your social circle, embrace other cultures and squeeze in a little more joy.

1960s: Jerry Williams represents black railway workers in the UK and helps them rise up the ranks.

Money, it turns out, was like sex - you thought of nothing else if you didn't have it and thought of other things if you did.
James Baldwin

October 28

When all we have are financial worries, nothing else counts in our lives. Every waking thought is spent on trying to find more money, recounting the money we have, schemes to stretch money further. With only this on our mind, our lives are the poorer. Money is important, but we cannot afford to let it dominate our lives while our friendships are left in the margins and our spirit is depleted. Keep money worries in proportion. A level head will balance out all your difficulties.

1987: Flip Fraser launches *Black Heroes in the Hall of Fame.* **London's first theatre celebration of black culture.**

Anticipate the good so that you may enjoy it.
Ethiopian proverb

October 29

You are entitled to all the riches of the universe and, believe me, they WILL come to you. Maybe not today, maybe not tomorrow, but soon. Don't dwell on the gloomy side of life. Or say, "it would be nice if..." Instead, say "It WILL be nice when..." If we do not realise the many joys that are promised to us, we may miss them and not realise it.

You don't know anything except what's there for you to see.
A. Baraka

October 30

Think of all the people who have come into your life over the past year. Did you think at the beginning of the year that you would have met any of them? Or think of all the strange twists that your life has taken? All these things are there, out of our line of vision. Open your eyes. Yes, but don't for one minute think that you can see even a tenth of what will happen in your life.

With our short sight we affect to take a comprehensive view of eternity. Our horizon is the universe.
Paul L. Dunbar

October 31

Look in the mirror, what do you see? Do you see a person who has lived through hardship as well as joy? Given love and received it? Made mistakes, and made amendments? A person that still has so much more to do and give? A person who still has much to enjoy, learn and experience? That is what stands in the mirror before you. A person with infinite possibilities. Can you really see all these things? Or do you only see a body in need of better care? A person who has failed and not fulfilled any goals? Look really hard.

1989: David Dinkins becomes the first black mayor of New York City.

Never work just for money or for power. They won't save your soul or help you sleep at night.
Miriam Wright Edelman

November 1

Pain, fear and anger are blindfolds which we put on ourselves. When we remove the blindfolds from the eyes of our spirit, then we can hope to feel joy, fulfilment and satisfaction. The unveiling of the spirit allows light to flood in.As we travel through life we are in touch with all parts of the universe, even if we do not know it. And the universe is in touch with us. Every dream, thought and wish we utter travels through it and comes back to us. The answer may not have been the one we had expected but the universe doesn't forget. Our SOS call may have gone out a day, a month, a year ago, or even longer — but it comes. Have the patience to wait for the reply.

1944: Sharon P. Dixon becomes the first African-American woman to be elected Mayor of Washington D.C.

I really, deeply believe that dreams do come true. Often they might not come when you want them. They come in their own time.
Diana Ross

November 2

1993: Established by Help the Aged, Swata, a group of elderly musicians, become the most popular band in Tanzania.

Love is positive energy which puts aside all of life's fears. When someone special stands by us, we are fearless and the possibilities are vast. The truth is that fearlessness was in us anyway, but sometimes we need to hear that loving voice whispering "yes, you can do it". We should treat those who have love for us as special. Like our parents. Their insight gives us faith and our faith allows us to be fearless in reaching the limitless potential that is within each and every one of us.

If I believe in me I can move mountains.

November 3

1980s: Black fashion icon Bruce Oldfield becomes Princess Diana's favourite designer.

Look around. Do you have friends — few or many? Relatives? Food? A home? YES? Well, give thanks, and, enjoy them in this moment. No one knows what will happen next. When things are gone we lament them. Take pleasure in the things you have, it doesn't stop you from wanting other things, different things, but value what you have in the here and now. The air that goes into your lungs, the rain that you say ruins your best clothes, all five of your senses that give you a variety of sensations. The sun, the moon and all the stars in the constellation. You are healthy and truly wealthy, realise that and give thanks.

Be bold and ask what you want.

November 4

Each of us deserves the best that life has to offer us, but the surest way not to get it is if we say nothing and allow it to pass us by. Be strong enough to say that "I want, I deserve..." Timidness gets you no part of the cake. Throw open your hands and what will fall into them will amaze you. But first you must believe wholeheartedly that it should be yours. We sometimes think that what we have in our hearts is too much or too big a gift to receive, or that we haven't worked hard enough to get it. Be bold enough to ask for what you want, and after uttering the wish believe that it will come to you.

1911: NAACP aims:
Abolish legal injustice against Negroes.

Stamp out racism.

Prevent lynchings, burnings, torturing.

Rights of citizenship for people of colour.

Equal accommodation in rail travel.

Fair schooling for black children.

Emancipate African-Americans.

November 5

Now you've got what you wanted, do you want more? We expect wealth to bring us happiness, peace and love, but instead it brings with it different problems. We expect money to be the end of all our worries, but it is only the beginning. You cannot be truly wealthy if fear and misery rule your life. There are too many things in life that are too precious, things that money can never buy. The sweetest love, for example.

1875: Benjamin 'Pap' Singleton leads nearly 7,500 black settlers from racism in Tennessee to build new communities in Kansas.

Count your blessings, name them one by one and it will surprise you what the Lord has done.

November 6

1990: Linbert Spencer launches the UK Agency for Economic Development, specialising in helping black businesses to gain funding and resources.

Most people want to be rich. The only thing that is stopping them is their state of mind. They think poor. They want to save, scrimp, cut corners. Wealth has as much to do with what is in your mind as what you have in your pocket. You want to be rich, think rich. They say that money attracts money. Then make sure your bank account is always in credit. The more you have, the more money it will attract. LITERALLY. If you want to be rich, do what the rich people do. Wear the type of clothes they wear and have the same attitude to life as they do. Change your consciousness from one of poverty to one of prosperity. Buy things of quality, do things with class and dream rich people's dreams.

Think like a queen.
Oprah Winfrey

November 7

1985: Gertrude Paul, organiser and founder of the West Indian Centre in Leeds, is given a *Caribbean Times Award* for services to the UK African-Caribbean community.

Real wealth is yours when you have love in your heart. Even in the midst of poverty, life continues. Joy and pain is felt, children are born and love is exchanged. Every day is a blessing and brings with it marvellous possibilities, no matter your predicament. Recognise REAL wealth, think it, live it, breathe it. Whoever you are and wherever you are, be determined to HAVE A NICE DAY.

Cast down your bucket where you are.
Booker T. Washington

November 8

Here you are in the midst of the greatest age, in a time where dreams are made possible and wishes come true. What period am I talking about? The age of you! Everything your eyes can see can be yours. Everything the sun touches is yours. Why wait for a mythical age to dawn when it has already dawned? From the moment you were conceived the age was coming into being. As you burst from your mother's womb and took your first breath, the age of you began. As you stand in the world and witness its beauty and see the achievements of mankind your era shifts and changes around you. Realise your kingdom, begin your reign, sit on your throne, don your crown. What are you waiting for?

1979: Carl T. Rowan becomes Editor of the *Oakland Tribune* in California. Four years later he buys the paper - the first African-American to own a major daily.

Poverty is slavery.
Somali proverb

November 9

Many great civilisations have believed in the power of dreams and that in the state of semi-consciousness, spirits from different worlds are able to communicate with each one of us. Certainly our dreams offer a freedom that reality does not share. Dreams allow us experiences that we would never dare in our waking hours. Our dreams speak to us in volumes. Do you listen or ignore them?

1947: Frank Yerby's *The Foxes of Harrow* is the first African-American novel to be made into a film by Hollywood.

My ancestors dream to me. Come and show me the magic blackness...
Maureen Ismay

November 10

1975: MPLA successfully drive out the reluctant Portuguese colonialists to achieve independence for Angola.

Seize the moment.
Seize the second.
Seize the minute.
Seize the hour.
Seize the day.
Seize the night.
Seize the week.
Seize the month.
Seize the year.
Seize the TIME!

When we give love, show compassion, bring joy and share experiences with one another, we make a deposit into the bank of the universe. The payment will surely come back to us with interest. When we give to friends or lovers we give back to ourselves. The universe keeps an account of everything that we do or say. The numbers are tallied and from time to time we get a pay-back. At times we are surprised at our "good fortune" — but really it is the payment for the deposit we have made some time ago. Invest in the world and it will make many profitable repayments, and you will never be bankrupt.

November 11

1921: Sadie T.M. Alexander (University of Pennsylvania), Eva B. Dykes (Radcliffe College) and Georgianna Rosa Simpson (University of Chicago) are the first black women to receive PhDs.

To pass something on to another is not to lose it but to invest it.

When we are at one with ourselves and the Creator all is well. If you cannot find love, peace, wisdom and understanding in your life, put right the relationship you have with the Creator. Meditate, pray, do what is needed to be rejoined to the source.

November 12

If you think you are beaten, you are,
if you think you dare not, you don't,
if you'd like to win, but think you can't,
it's almost a cinch you won't.

If you think you'll lose, you're lost,
for out in the world we find
success begins with a fellow's will -
it's all in the state of mind.

If you think you are outclassed, you are,
you've got to think high to rise.
You've just got to be sure of yourself
before you can win the prize.

Life's battles don't always go
to the stronger or faster man,
but sooner or later the man who wins
is the one who thinks he can.

1771: James Somerset demands his freedom, and that of the other 20,000 black servants in London.

My relationship with God is part of my relationship with man. Failure in one will cause failure with the other.

November 13

Allow the spirit to flow through your body. Make yourself a vessel for what the Creator has in store for you. We have ALL been made for a special purpose, a purpose you and only you can achieve. Until you are one with the Creator you cannot know your purpose. When you have come to the understanding, your life will bring joy, fulfilment and love to yourself and others.

1789: Olaudah Equiano, first political leader of black British community.

Blow your own trumpet and you'll simply disturb the neighbours. Blow Gods' trumpet, and you'll wake the dead.

November 14

If you had to save a handful of things from an inferno, what would they be? Everything you should need can be carried in your heart and in your mind. The tools you need to build your life, make changes and decisions, are all in you. The tools that give you joy and amusement are with you too. In fact the most important thing you should want to save from the fire is yourself. Everything else can be replaced. If you always carry the tools of life in your heart you will be content to start up home again and again.

Happiness is not having many things, but needing few.

November 15

If you call yourself a queen, show your class. Queens do not slouch around; walk like a queen. Queens demand the best and will not settle for anything less. You shouldn't either. Queens do not settle for poor treatment — neither should you. Queens know they have a right to be heard and know what they have to say is valid — SO SHOULD YOU. The Queen bows to no man. Neither should you.

The earth yields her fruit to you, learn how to fill your hands.

November 16

The Creator has given us everything we need to live a truly wonderful life, those great and powerful gifts which enable us to escape the destructive forces in the world. Aspire to add goodness to faith, to your goodness add knowledge, to your knowledge add common sense, to your common sense add endurance, to your endurance add godliness. These are the qualities you need, and if you have them in abundance they will make you active and effective in your life.

1972: Chinua Achebe wins the Commonwealth Poetry Prize.

Every knot has an unraveller in God.
Egyptian proverb

November 17

1964: Louis Armstrong records *Hello Dolly* and grosses more from it than any black artist has earned from one record.

Is your heart a place where you would want your children to live in? Is it a warm place, a comfortable place? Does it offer shelter? Is it clean and pure? Does it welcome them home every day with love? Your heart is the foundation of everything you say and do, make sure it is a little heaven for your children. They need all the love they can get.

A man who does not think far ahead in whatever he does, is sure to be troubled by worries much closer at hand.
Confucious

November 18

1962: Patsy Robertson, a black woman living in the UK, is among the first women recruited to the British Foreign Service when it is established.

Knowledge Reigns Supreme Over Nearly Everyone

Joy is limitless. You have only savoured a touch of it, you have so much more joy to encounter! As joy has no limits, do not restrict your joy. Take joy to YOUR limit, then double it and then multiply it an infinite number of times. You will discover that just as joy has no limits, you yourself are limitless when it comes to the amount of joy you can consume.

November 19

1996: George Weah, the world's top soccer player, pays for the entire squad of his home country, Liberia, to take part in the African Nations Cup when their government cannot afford it.

Laughter is healthy; its absence causes heart attacks.

When was the last time you had a good laugh? A good, shoulder-jerking, side-splitting, uninhibited laugh? It isn't illegal or outlawed yet. And even if it was, we would still be laughing, if only in secret. If laughing was contraband, crime syndicates would smuggle it in and make a fortune selling it on street corners. Not only is laughing NOT illegal, but it is clinically proven to help boost the immune system and prevents depression, by encouraging the brain to produce chemicals that lift us up to a natural high. It's official: laughter gets you stoned. So go ahead, laugh. It costs you nothing!

November 20

Some people can cry because of the contents of a book, film, play, picture or painting and there are others who cannot cry, even in the face of human tragedy or bereavement. Weeping is a natural part of the healing process. Tears give us an outlet for our emotions — pain, anger fear, joy, thankfulness. Sometimes life simply moves you to tears.

1972: The Harder they Come, starring Jimmy Cliff is the first Jamaican feature film.

God lent us his property here so that we too should lend what we have to our neighbours.
Swahili proverb

November 21

We are too ready to settle for second best in our lives in terms of relationships, jobs, prosperity and even health.. Just because we do not display any symptoms we consider ourselves to be healthy. But true health is a measure of inner joy, peace and exuberance. Wealth is what we have when both our body and spirit are in harmony. How can you gain wealth when you wake up feeling dull and stay that way all through the day? How can you reap the whirlwind when your energy is low? When we allow the powerful, rejuvenating energy which is within us all to surge through our bodies there is no limit to how much more healthier and consequently profitable our lives will become.

1977: Harold Mood receives the Musgrave Gold Medal, Jamaica's most prestigious cultural award.

No matter where you come from, as long as you're a black man/ woman, you're an African. Even if your complexion is high, or low, or in-between, you're an African.
Peter Tosh

November 22

1897: African-American J.L. Love receives the patent for the pencil sharpener.

Not everything in life works "according to plan". Things take a longer or shorter period of time than we initially thought, and some stages we find aren't necessary at all. But if you don't make a plan, chances are you will never get anything done. A plan directs you to your goal, without which your life is without purpose. Plan your day, week, month and year carefully. Put your life in the right direction.

I used to moan that I was so poor I didn't have any shoes on my feet, until I met someone who didn't have any feet.

November 23

1982: Jamaican born Val McCalla launches The Voice newspaper, soon to become the UK's largest selling black weekly.

The sooner you become attuned to life's timetable the happier you will be. Patience is the key. With patience, many of those obstacles you face will seem less daunting. Patience is your guarantee that what you don't have now will come eventually. Why waste your time trying to fix life? It isn't necessary. With a patient attitude both your spiritual and physical health are at their best and you are better able to reap the harvest of your life.

It's not that we plan to fail, but we fail to plan.

November 24

You don't need to do anything to become
   worthy.
You already are.
You don't even have to discover or define what
gives   you your worthiness.
You can feel that you are worthy
Even in your darkest hour
worthiness is an indisputable fact.
You are worthy because you are.

1984: Earl Robinson MBE Joe Williams Lionel Morrison all received *Caribbean Times Awards* for their contribution to the Community.

A patient man has all the wealth in the world.
Jabo

November 25

The saying tells us that "money isn't everything" — but it certainly is something. It counts for a lot, and gives us a lot of freedom. It allows us to accomplish so much and enables us to be free of things we have to do in order to do the things we want to do. Nurture a healthy respect for money. Not resentment or worship, but a healthy acknowledgement of its place within our life. When we respect money we are more likely to approach it and all things financial in a healthy and constructive way. We learn to be intelligent in the way we handle it. When money is combined with common sense, intuition and creativity, there is no telling what good can be achieved.

1980: Ann Thompson is appointed West Indian Community Librarian by the City of Westminister and immediately purchases 6000 black books.

Everybody loves a winner, but if you lose... you lose alone.

November 26

1865-66: Chief John Aggrey is the first African ruler to organize protests against the British colonialists on the Gold Coast.

*Come correct with love and not hatred
And surely goodness and mercy will follow you.*

To have peace of mind — let your thoughts flow, don't dictate them. Let them go where they want to go.

To have peace in your emotions — stop trying to manipulate them. Learn from your feelings, acknowledge them, celebrate them.

To have physical peace — stop fighting with life. Don't push your body beyond comfortable limits. Rest the body, but exercise it.

To have peace with others — don't fight with them. Do your own thing, go your own way. Embrace those who walk with you. If at times you walk alone, accept it. Maintain a "portable paradise" within yourself.

When you are not contantly battling, you will finally find peace.

November 27

1987: UK based Nigerian, Mr Oshin, a top watchmaker, has been a proprietor of his successful business for over 40 years.

*Lift up your heads!
Be proud! be brave!*

Let compassion be your temple.
Let faith be your fuel.
Let honest living be your guide book.
Let modesty be the rules of observance.
Let tolerance be the faith you keep.
Right conduct the path you walk.
Truth the house in which you keep your thoughts.
Good deeds your prayer.
As myriads of waves arise from the same ocean
But ultimately come back to merge in the same water,
So do myriads of forms
Rise from the same vast form of God
And ultimately come back.

Sikh belief

November 28

Catch up with your good. As is the divine way our good has gone before us, it has gotten there before we have. We have become lazy and slow if we have not caught up with it. If we are to begin to enjoy the abundance we must be less lethargic, or else our goodness will always be out of reach. When we become locked into a way of thinking that we have always had hard times and make do, we will always have just that — nothing! When we are asleep to our opportunities with aliveness, we catch up to and grasp onto our goodness.

1987: Spike Lee developed 'guerilla filmmaking' with his debut movie *She's Gotta Have It*, which he funded with his credit card. (By any means necessary.)

You must speak straight so that your words may go as sunlight into our hearts.
Chiricahua chief

November 29

The person with a rich consciousness and the one with a poor consciousness are not on the same mental road. "The way to abundance is a one-way street." You are either heading towards abundance and prosperity or you are going in another direction — towards want and hardship. There is an ample supply divinely planned and put there by the Creator. The rich person is harnessing rich thoughts and will eventually gain rich surroundings. The world of the richly minded person is that of crystallised thought and deed. Sooner rather than later they are bound to reap the harvest of their words and thoughts.

Arise courageous - unafraid!

November 30

We never ask a person who has failed "what is the secret to your failure?" In pursuit of the secret door to success, everyone wants to know how a RICH AND SUCCESSFUL person achieved their aspirations. Secrets to success are many, but what every successful person agrees on is that, without self realisation, faith, courage and enthusiasm, success will always be elusive.

December 1

They say that a good friend is better than pocket money, because when the money's gone your good friends are still around. Make sure that you value the friendship of those close to you. Show them that you care for them as they care for you.

December 2

If we are generous with our love we benefit from the abundance of life. If we use love as a tool and only give it when we approve of situations we are destined to see life as an obstacle course and others will enter into a contest in order to gain our love. If we give love indiscriminately we are likely to be drained and receive nothing in return. But when we have found balance in ourselves, then we learn one of the greatest lessons life can teach us: "How much we love is as important as who we love."

1946: Ann Petry's *The Street* sells over a million copies, the first African-American book to do so.

If you know what life is worth, you will look for yours on earth.
Bob Marley

December 3

All that is life — good fortune, misfortune, joy and disappointment — are vibrations. We are vibrating in synchronisation either with what we are used to or what we are aspiring to. If you are on the same vibration as misfortune, bad luck and difficulty, then that is all you will meet on your path. But when you vibrate to joy, love and fulfilment, all your life will be filled with pleasant and positive experiences. When we actively seek to vibrate on a positive plane, we become more in tune with the good that is in the world for us.

1906: James Perters is the first black man to play rugby for England.

You can't win unless you learn how to lose.
Kareem Abdul Jabbar

December 4

You rank up there next to the world's finest. Without a doubt. You didn't realise that? All this time you thought you were Miss Average and you achieved only average in everything. Now that you know that you are amongst the best, what will you achieve?

December 5

I can see clearly now, the rain has gone. I can now see all the obstacles in my way. Now that I am truly *of* the Creator, my inner vision bathes my life in pure light and banishes the fog of confusion which previously caused me to stumble. I can see clearly now, that my fears and limitations were a result of distorted vision. I can see the truth clearly now and the truth is I AM IN CONTROL OF ME.

December 6

By a combination of historical subservience and conditioning, so many of us are unaware of our own achievements. If we do not recognise and appreciate our achievements, who else will? If we do not strive to attain and recognise the goals that were denied to our forbears then they have given their lives in vain.

1990: Joseph Abraham is made the first black Mayor of Waltham Forest, London.

Never stop dreaming of a better life.

December 7

Think of your favourite sport: netball, tennis, basketball. Think how much you enjoy taking part. Think of your feeling of elation when you win. How much more should we enjoy playing the game of life? The stakes are high and the goal is ultimate: happiness. The rules are sometimes complicated, but the referee is always fair. In this game it is important to maintain your physical peak, because every muscle and tendon is tested and our capabilities are stretched. In the game of life our main opponent is always ourselves. If you are the master of yourself, you are bound to win.

1864: Herbert Macauley founds the first political party in Nigeria and campaigns hard for self-rule. He is commemorated on the Naira, currency of Nigeria.

If we are afraid to insist we are right, then what?
June Jordan

December 8

The headwrap is back in style. Everywhere I look, I see sistas wearing them loud and proud. Each time we throw open our cupboard and choose our garments we are entering into an age-old dialogue. Each item of clothing we choose speaks to us and about us. The colours we prefer and the combinations in which we wear them, are confessions of the soul. Choose clothes that speak of your spirit, mind and emotions. Make your body the temple of the spirit and the garments you place upon it, the echo of its voice.

You can't solve your problem until you're aware that the problem exists.

December 9

He says he is sorry and asks you to take him back. And, despite your better judgment, you're considering it. Consider how he betrayed you. Consider how it nearly drove you out of your head. Consider all those hurtful things that were said. And now, he says he loves you. And, despite your better judgment, you're considering taking him back. Okay, but first, tell him to consider how many tears you shed and tell him that if he means what he's now saying then he should prove it. Tell him to cry you a river, like all the rivers you've cried over him, then MAYBE you'll consider it.

Respect commands itself. It can neither be given nor withheld when it is due.
Eldridge Cleaver

December 10

Take time to consider life's contradictions. What is their purpose? It may be that you were on the wrong course all along. In which case the contradiction is a red 'warning' flag to abandon this route. It may be that we just need to find a balance. In this way we are focused yet our minds are open. When we are balanced we always find that there are options open to us.

1995: Stan Collymore is transferred from Nottingham Forest to Liverpool for a record £8.5 million, in a season when the four most expensive soccer players in the UK are all black.

Can you afford not to invest in your child?

December 11

Life is chaotic because of the many roles we have to juggle: wife, husband, mother, father, work mate, brother sister, niece, nephew, grandparent, friend, acquaintance, friend of a friend. They all make demands on our time, energy and strength. So much time that we barely find time to think. We would save ourselves a great deal of grief in life, if we just stopped to think for a minute and organise our affairs.

1899: African-American G. F. Grant receives the patent for the golf tee.

Life is just a short walk from the cradle to the grave - and it sure behoves us to be kind to one another along the way.
Alice Childeress

December 12

Food plays an important part in our lives. We love it so much that we have even given it a spiritual name, "soul food". Soul food is food that nourishes the parts other foods fail to reach. Food that is enriched with a blessing and the collective energy that created it as well as the natural nutrients found in the ingredients. Soul food is any healthy meal made with love, care and enthusiasm.

December 13

Don't Quit.
When things go wrong as they sometimes will,
When the road you're trodding seems all uphill,
When the funds are low and the debts high,
And you want to smile,
But you have to sigh,
Rest if you must, but don't quit.
Success is failure turned inside out,
The silver tint of the clouds of doubt,
And you never can tell how close you are,
It may be near when
It seems afar.
So, stick to the fight
When you're hardest hit —
It's when things go wrong
That you mustn't quit.

December 14

You are a tiny part of the universe, but as vital to the cosmos as the sun and moon and stars with which you share your space. Each of us stamp our unique print on the 'history of the world' and in millions of years yours will still be there for generations to marvel. Now, you may have all the feminine charms that man admires, but when future generations look back to get as much information as they can on the rich and diverse history, struggles, conditions, and accomplishments of women of colour, what they will find is whether you were a REAL sista who cared about your sistas. That's what makes the world go round.

1987: African-American Dr Carson, successfully separates Siamese twins joined at the head.

The true journey of discovery comes not in seeking new landscapes, but in having new eyes.

December 15

When we pray, hope or speak, we limit ourselves; when we love, share and give we limit ourselves. Let today be the first day when you place no limits on what you hope for, what you speak of and what you pray for. Let today be a day when you open wide your arms, your heart and your mind. Place no limits on what comes into your life and no limits on the energy you expend. Embrace every new situation as it comes and let it teach you about yourself, the world and others. Do not set rigid timetables, as time is infinite and flows continuously. Above all do not restrict what it is that you think the Creator can give to you, for the supply is endless and the intent is pure.

1988: Loose Ends become the first black British group to successfully export its sound to the U.S.

If A equals success, then the formula is A=X+Y+Z. X is hard work, Y is work harder, Z is live good.

December 16

1992: Dr Mae Jemison becomes the first black woman in space.

A new earth rises, another world is born. Peace is written in the sky. With beauty full of healing pulsing in our veins we, a new generation, rise and take control.

Being black and being a woman means one thing: YOU HAVE POTENTIAL. That's right — YOU. Neither poverty, hunger, nor inhumane treatment or any other disadvantages can keep you from your potential. Nobody but yourself can stop you from demonstrating your exceptional determination, resilience and intellectual ability. Therefore do something with your life. Any woman can overcome obstacles if she possesses a healthy dose of faith in her own potential. Rejuvenate the energy of your potential and discover a whole new perspective on what you can achieve in life.

December 17

1950: Gwendolyn Brooks becomes the first black female writer to win a Pulitzer Prize for her collection of poems *Annie Allen.*

Getting wisdom is the most important thing you can do.
Proverbs 4 v.7

Every meditation is a moment in itself. I hear my inner voice, so I know who is talking. I know what we're talking about and why. I know why my inner voice can't stop saying this same thing to me. Some urgency accompanies the words. Something important is going on, something is reaching out to touch me. If I listen carefully, I will hear my heart's desire and if I consider the words deeply, I will have the solution.

December 18

We have all had times when our lives flow as naturally as laughter, when we are at our best and everything is done with great ease. Nothing can put us off our stride. We are relaxed, focused and effective. We are open to love and all of life's blessings. Then there are those days when nothing seems to go right at all. Days which make us feel like the Creator has abandoned us. These days are mean to test our faith. I believe I can make it through days like these. How strong is your faith?

1875: Dr Carter G. Woodson born. Destined to be a great black historian and scholar. He founded the Association for the Study of Negro Life & History.

When God shuts a door for us, he will open another door.
Swahili proverb

December 19

We intend to express our individual dark-skinned selves without fear or shame... We know we are beautiful. And ugly too... We build our temples for tomorrow, strong as we know how, and we stand on the top of the mountain, free within ourselves. **Langston Hughes**

1959: Ruth Bowen establishes her talent agency in New York with artists such as Aretha Franklin, Gladys Knight and the Pips, Sammy Davis Jr.

I am a wisp of energy flung from the core of the universe housed in a temple of flesh and bones and blood.
Mari Evans

December 20

1957: Alex Tetteh-Lartey composes the national anthem of Ghana. He also presents the BBC flagship African radio programme, *Focus on Africa.*

We share one love, one heart, one destiny. Isn't it about time we all got together?

We live in a time when the distinction between rich and poor is so great the gulf seems almost insurmountable. One side of the world has so much that they have it to burn whilst the rest of the world is constantly at starvation's door. Too often people of colour believe that we are life's poorer cousins. In fact, the opposite is true. We have in us a richness of spirit which is unique and surpasses all material wealth, and a sense of unity and communal spirit handed down from our ancestors. We can be doubly blessed, not cursed, because of whence we came.

December 21

1871: Fisk Jubilee Singers tour Europe to raise money for their black college in the U.S.

If you want quick results, you'll never complete your task. And if you only see petty gains, you can never achieve things.

When we make affirmations we bring our thoughts into words and, through faith, into being. Affirmations focus the mind.

December 22

For Prosperity: The Creator is my continuous supply; what I need will come to me in a perfect form.

For Purpose: What is needed to be done by me I will do as I come upon it on my journey, what is for me will bring me joy and satisfaction.

For Faith: I am of the Creator and what flows from the Creator flows through me.

For Health: As I am of the Creator what is healthy and pure is what is in me.

For Guidance: I am in tune with both my logic and intuition as I know that they come both from the Creator and work for my benefit.

1862: Richard Him presents petition to the House of Commons demanding civil rights for Jamaicans.

Many people, many cultures, many languages - with one thing in common, the yearning to breathe free. Common ground.
Jesse Jackson

December 23

Libation

For the Motherland cradle of civilisation.
For the ancestors and their indomitable spirit.
For the elders from whom we can learn much.
For our youth who represent the promise for
tomorrow.
For the people, the original people.
For the struggle, and in remembrance of those
who   have struggled on our behalf.
For Umojo, the principle of unity which should
guide us in all we do.
For the Creator, who provides all things great and
small.

1996: According to British government figures, young black people are LESS likely to commit crimes than their white counterparts.

Respect your elders no matter how old you get.

December 24

1966: Kwanzaa established by Dr Paul Maulana Karenga, a Black Studies professor in the U.S. Kwanzaa is a cultural festival. A black alternative to another white Xmas.

Kwanzaa
Imani - Faith

When there seems little else option in life, we fall on our knees and pray. You can almost touch the subsequent release of anguish as it leaves your body. We rise to our feet, feeling replenished, confident that we can face whatever life may hold for us. If prayer can make you feel this positive, you should pray every day.

December 25

1948: Caribbean born London resident Barron Baker, welcomes Jamaican immigrants from the SS Empire Windrush and helps them find homes and jobs in the UK.

Kwanzaa
Umoja -
Unity.

As the lyrics to a hit tune go, "We are family". And to that family circle we bring our rich diversity, talents and characteristics. Like every family we have our differences, our disputes, but like all good families we know at the end of the day that we are tied together with the bonds of blood. Our strength comes from being in that family. It is our duty to ensure that as a family, both by blood and in spirit, we keep ourselves well, mentally, physically and spiritually. As we would not deliberately hurt ourselves we must not wish any harm on our brothas and sistas.

December 26

We are a creative people. Everything we do, think or touch we turn into art. It may not be displayed in museums or exhibited in galleries, we may not even think of all we do as creative, but it is. When we have pride and gain enjoyment from our work we enhance the task with spirit. When we make a meal for those that we love we create a mood, when we share our home with others we create a warm environment. When we tell tales of old myths and modern anecdotes we invoke the magic of words. When we rest and sleep we invoke the spirit of harmony and balance. Creativity crackles around us like electricity, and we don't even notice because we take it for granted.

1992 : Mrs Lorrette William's settles out of court, her case against the Home Office.

Kwanzaa
Kujichagulia -
Self-determination.

December 27

Generations have fought in order for us to get where we are now, and it is vital that when we pass the baton on to the next generation we have made equally significant strides. Without hope we perish. Hope for our children will be our own advancement. That is what keeps every generation reaching for the skies. Make sure that your only direction is up.

Cloud Caulker's Trade Union Society buys shipyard and railways, by collectively pooling money and resources.

Kwanzaa
Ujima -
Collective work and responsibility.

December 28

1957: Tuskegee, Alabama. Black people boycott white owned shops, as a protest against the gerrymandering of local electoral districts to reduce black voting power.

Kwanzaa
Ujamaa -
Co-operative economics.

Ain't got no mother ain't got no father, sister or brother. Ain't got no friends. Ain't got no home, ain't got no clothes, ain't got no money. Ain't got no food, ain't got no drink. Ain't got no class, ain't got no culture. Ain't got no silver spoon in my mouth. Ain't got no lovin'. Ain't got no lover. Ain't got no education. But what do I care? When I've got my head and my brains and my mouth and my hands and my legs and my fingers. I've got my soul, I've got my smile and I've got my faith. I've got LIFE. My future lies in my hands, there is no better time for me to make it a good one than the present.

December 29

1981: Jamaica issues a postage stamp to honour its most famous son, Bob Marley. The stamps sell out in hours and become a collector's item worldwide.

Kwanzaa
Nia - *Purpose*

Everybody deserves a smile from you, every day of the week. Especially you. Because every day is the season of goodwill. Goodwill to everybody, especially you. Just when you're about to frown, disarm people with a smile. Show that you're coming from a higher level. When in doubt, show your class.

December 30

There are those who would have us believe that by the colour of our skin, our future is limited. But the pages of history are peppered with men and women who have this same 'limitation' and have carved out empires, amassed fortunes for themselves and brought about revolutionary changes. How could we possibly be limited by colour when our destinies are as diverse as the many beautiful, radiant shades of our skin?

1997: The largest number of black graduates receive their degrees from British universities and celebrate at the first ever black graduation ball in London

Duppy know who fe frighten Jamaican proverb

December 31

Stop and think. It is not too late. Tomorrow is a new day, a new year. The lessons of the last 365 days teach that you and you alone are responsible for your destiny. It is your choice. The only thing you cannot choose is not to choose: that's a choice in itself. Just as 'do the right thing' was the battle cry of yesterday, 'make the right choice' is the flavour of tomorrow. Go on, make the right resolution, you know it will do you good.

1997: Pop legend Jimi Hendrix is honoured with a prestigious blue plaque at his former home in London

Fowl run from hawk but nyam cockroach Jamaican proverb

Week 1

I will turn my positive thoughts into positive actions

_____

_____

_____

_____

_____

_____

_____

_____

_____

_____

_____

_____

_____

_____

_____

_____

Week2

Today I shall be patient - honest!

_____

_____

_____

_____

_____

_____

_____

_____

_____

_____

_____

_____

_____

_____

_____

_____

_____

_____

_____

_____

Week 3

I am open to new ideas

Week 4

I celebrate my beauty and the beauty of my culture

_____

_____

_____

_____

_____

_____

_____

_____

_____

_____

_____

_____

_____

_____

_____

_____

_____

_____

_____

Week 5

I celebrate all that I am

_____

_____

_____

_____

_____

_____

_____

_____

_____

_____

_____

_____

_____

_____

_____

_____

_____

_____

_____

_____

_____

_____

Week 6

I have everything that I need

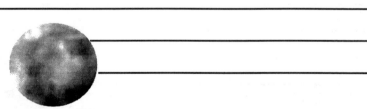

Week 7

Everyday, in every way, I am getting stronger

_____

_____

_____

_____

_____

_____

_____

_____

_____

_____

_____

_____

_____

_____

_____

_____

_____

_____

_____

_____

_____

_____

_____

Week 8

I will consider what I did yesterday and do better today and tomorrow

_____

_____

_____

_____

_____

_____

_____

_____

_____

_____

_____

_____

_____

_____

_____

_____

_____

_____

_____

_____

_____

Week 9

Doubts have no place in my thinking and feeling

_____

_____

_____

_____

_____

_____

_____

_____

_____

_____

_____

_____

_____

_____

_____

_____

_____

_____

_____

Week 10

These fears no longer have a home in my life

_____

_____

_____

_____

_____

_____

_____

_____

_____

_____

_____

_____

_____

_____

_____

_____

_____

_____

_____

_____

Week11

I can weather the storm

_____

_____

_____

_____

_____

_____

_____

_____

_____

_____

_____

_____

_____

_____

_____

_____

_____

_____

_____

_____

_____

_____

_____

Week12

I cherish myself in so many different ways

_____

_____

_____

_____

_____

_____

_____

_____

_____

_____

_____

_____

_____

_____

_____

_____

_____

_____

_____

_____

_____

Week13

This week I will DO:

Week14

My life is a series of adventures

Week15

My sacrifices are for the sake of my achievements

_____

_____

_____

_____

_____

_____

_____

_____

_____

_____

_____

_____

_____

_____

_____

_____

_____

_____

_____

_____

_____

_____

_____

Week16

I reclaim my heritage

_____

_____

_____

_____

_____

_____

_____

_____

_____

_____

_____

_____

_____

_____

_____

_____

_____

_____

_____

_____

_____

_____

Week17

My inner voice speaks to me

Week18

I have accomplished every goal

_____

_____

_____

_____

_____

_____

_____

_____

_____

_____

_____

_____

_____

_____

_____

_____

_____

_____

_____

_____

Week19

I create the me I want to be in many ways

_____

_____

_____

_____

_____

_____

_____

_____

_____

_____

_____

_____

_____

_____

_____

_____

_____

_____

_____

_____

_____

_____

Week 20

I realise all my blessings

_____

_____

_____

_____

_____

_____

_____

_____

_____

_____

_____

_____

_____

_____

_____

_____

_____

_____

_____

_____

_____

_____

_____

Week21

I have learned beautiful things

Week22

My prayers bring wisdom

_____

_____

_____

_____

_____

_____

_____

_____

_____

_____

_____

_____

_____

_____

_____

_____

_____

_____

_____

_____

_____

_____

Week23

Learning to love, I have learned to live

Week24

I never stop dreaming of good things

Week25

I have resolved several issues

Week26

I do not wait for opportunities, I make them

_____

_____

_____

_____

_____

_____

_____

_____

_____

_____

_____

_____

_____

_____

_____

_____

_____

_____

_____

Week27

Negative vibes and I have parted company

Week28

I share my experience and knowledge

Week29

I make the world smile in so many ways

_____

_____

_____

_____

_____

_____

_____

_____

_____

_____

_____

_____

_____

_____

_____

_____

_____

_____

_____

_____

_____

Week30

I am rich in love and well being

_____

_____

_____

_____

_____

_____

_____

_____

_____

_____

_____

_____

_____

_____

_____

_____

_____

_____

_____

_____

_____

Week31

I become stronger everyday

Week32

Every now and then I take a little time for myself

_____

_____

_____

_____

_____

_____

_____

_____

_____

_____

_____

_____

_____

_____

_____

_____

_____

_____

_____

_____

_____

Week33

Behold, the many visions I have had today

Week34

I acknowledge the black heroes in my hall of fame

_____

_____

_____

_____

_____

_____

_____

_____

_____

_____

_____

_____

_____

_____

_____

_____

_____

_____

_____

_____

_____

_____

Week35

I have discovered a diamond in the rough - me!

_____

_____

_____

_____

_____

_____

_____

_____

_____

_____

_____

_____

_____

_____

_____

_____

_____

_____

_____

_____

_____

Week36

I share more with other people of colour than I realised

_____

_____

_____

_____

_____

_____

_____

_____

_____

_____

_____

_____

_____

_____

_____

_____

_____

_____

_____

_____

Week37

I shall succeed.

Week38

I am not afraid to work hard for what I need

_____

_____

_____

_____

_____

_____

_____

_____

_____

_____

_____

_____

_____

_____

_____

_____

_____

_____

_____

_____

Week39

My imagination takes me to places I have never been before

_____

_____

_____

_____

_____

_____

_____

_____

_____

_____

_____

_____

_____

_____

_____

_____

_____

_____

_____

_____

_____

_____

_____

Week 40

I can heal my wounds

_____

_____

_____

_____

_____

_____

_____

_____

_____

_____

_____

_____

_____

_____

_____

_____

_____

_____

_____

_____

_____

Week 41

I show my class for all to see

Week42

The beauty of my spirit radiates in so many ways

Week 43

I still have a lot to learn

_____

_____

_____

_____

_____

_____

_____

_____

_____

_____

_____

_____

_____

_____

_____

_____

_____

_____

_____

_____

_____

_____

_____

_____

_____

Week44

I stay in touch with my soul

Week 45

I have made these improvements in my appearance

_____

_____

_____

_____

_____

_____

_____

_____

_____

_____

_____

_____

_____

_____

_____

_____

_____

_____

_____

Week46

I begin my day with a prayer

Week47

I have gained respect

Week48

I love life more than I love my possessions

_____

_____

_____

_____

_____

_____

_____

_____

_____

_____

_____

_____

_____

_____

_____

_____

_____

_____

_____

_____

_____

_____

Week 49

I think only healthy thoughts

Week50

I discover my inner beauty